Narcissistic Abuse Recovery

"Healing is not an overnight process. It is a daily cleansing of pain; it is a daily healing of your life."

Leon Brown

Table of Contents

Chapter 01: Introduction 5

    What to expect 6

    The big promise 7

    How to prepare to break free and heal from narcissistic abuse. 8

Chapter 02: Recognizing The Abusive Narcissist 12

    Who or what is a narcissist? 13

    The narcissist's false self and true self: 14

    What is narcissistic abuse? 16

    Different types of abuse to become aware of: 17

    Can empaths be narcissists too? 17

Chapter 03: What You May Not Know About Narcissism and NPD 20

    The Cause Of Narcissism 20

    What is NPD? 22

    Different types of narcissists 26

    What are some traits and symptoms of a narcissist? 26

    Types of extreme narcissists 31

    Traits of perfect targets for narcissists 33

Chapter 04: Tools of manipulation 35

    1. Gaslighting 35

    2. Avoiding accountability at all costs. 35

    3. Name-calling 36

    4. Covert and overt threats. 36

    5. Projection. 37

    6. Love-bombing and devaluation. 38

- 7. Triangulation. 38
- 8. Aggressive blows disguised as jokes. 39
- 9. Control. 39

Chapter 05: The science and psychology behind narcissistic relationships 41
- Your brain on trauma 41
- Why the emotional and psychological abuse? 42
- The cycle of abuse 44
- Idealization and love-bombing: 44
- Devaluation: 45
- The Discard: 46

Chapter 06: Narcissism at work and in relationships 49
- Narcissistic parents 49
- Narcissistic partners and how to free yourself How to break up with a narcissist 54
- Narcissism at work 55

Chapter 07: How Past Wounds Make Us Susceptible To Toxic Narcissists 57
- What is trauma? 58
- Five ways Abusive narcissists get to you 61

Chapter 08: Healing Trauma and permanently detaching 64
- What is detachment? 64
- Change begins with you. 65
- The six steps of your recovery 67
- Step One: Learn grounding techniques and self-soothing methods. 67
- Step Two: Allow yourself to be angry and grieve. 69
- Step Three: Stop researching obsessively on narcissism. 70
- Step Four: Develop your self-esteem. 71
- Step Five: Incorporate movement into your daily routine. 71

Step Six: Work on reconnecting with your passion and purpose in life. _____ 72

Five self-care suggestions that are integral to your complete healing and transformation _____ 72

Building your immunity and Identity after narcissistic abuse _____ 78

Chapter 09: No contact _____ 80

What No contact is and what it isn't _____ 80

Why we focus on remaining in No Contact _____ 82

Here's how to apply No Contact immediately _____ 82

Sticking to your No Contact Rule _____ 84

When a full No Contact isn't possible, what then? _____ 84

Chapter 10: 3 Steps To Reclaiming Your Power _____ 86

1. Take back your story and rewrite it. _____ 86

2. Forgive yourself. _____ 88

3. Rebuild your self-image and recognize your true worth. _____ 88

Educational Resources _____ 91

Chapter 01: Introduction

A few years back, I decided to embark on a journey that would ultimately change my life. I signed up to get professional therapy and joined a small forum that was recommended to me where survivors of psychological abuse gathered to support each other. This was a big move for me and somewhat awkward at first because I couldn't tell how this would enable me to get rid of the depression, low self-esteem and cycles of pain that I was going through. But the therapist that was treating me suggested it and quite frankly I was desperate to have a fresh start in life.

You see my story, like so many other survivors, was full of hidden psychological hurts. I realized I was carrying on a generational legacy of psychological abuse that was being passed down from generation to generation for who knows how long. The concept of love that I grew up with and experienced with my parents led me into intimate relationships and friendships that only perpetuated psychological abuse.

I had a father who was a cold, calculating control freak, and nothing I did was ever good enough for him. My mother, on the other hand, was always too warm, giving, needy, shy, and "too sensitive" according to my dad. He would often swap between mocking his wife's sensitivities my sub-par qualities. Even when I thought I had done really well (for example when I got a medal in a swimming competition), he still had countless of reasons to explain how I didn't live up to what he expected of me. My mother tried to leave my father at one point but soon got sucked back into the marriage. I even recall a time where they were sleeping in two separate bedrooms and was pretty sure it was the end of the marriage. No words were exchanged for weeks, and then slowly, my mother started exchanging warm, affectionate giggles. She got a new watch, started doing date nights again and the rest was history.

For a while, I thought this was the norm for all families. But as I grew into my teens, it started becoming even more evident that my family was very dysfunctional, and there was nothing healthy about the parental care I had received.

Each time I would start a romantic relationship, it wouldn't be too long before I found myself feeling like a human yo-yo. To my family members, I was more like the human punching bag that everyone enjoyed playing with, and even though I always felt something was off, it wasn't until my mid-twenties where I finally had enough. At first, the few people I confided in only made me feel worse - like I was paranoid, needy, and overthinking things. Perhaps you've experienced something similar?

It's tough to explain something in words that most people can barely resonate with because unless you have specific terms to describe the actions of a hidden abuser, most people will say you sound a bit crazy and unstable. Which is why I decided to do some Google research and eventually landed on a site that helped me get some professional help. Along that harrowing and intense journey, I learned some eye-opening truths about psychological abuse, which led me to the creation of this book.

As I continue to journey in life as a survivor and educate myself on this topic, it is my intention that the information I share with others can better empower them to step into their own power and heal their lives permanently.

Whether your hidden abuse comes from a romantic relationship, parents, in-laws, an employer, or whatever else the case might be for you, know that you are in the right place. Take the information contained in this book and apply it compassionately and diligently for it is the guidebook that can lead you to a life of freedom, empowerment, and self-worth.

What to expect

Abuse can take many forms. This includes mental, physical, sexual, financial, emotional, and even spiritual abuse. Most types of abuse are invisible, but they leave long-lasting scars on the survivors and deep wounds on the victims. What I am going to focus on mostly is providing you with a wealth of information on narcissistic abuse. But what's essential for you to note is that gathering the knowledge alone will not help you heal. Healing is about gaining awareness and then taking action on the acquired knowledge.

This book is specifically designed to help you reclaim your personal power so you can permanently heal. It will empower you to take full responsibility for your life and to change the current perception you carry of yourself.

You'll be able to design a life of meaning for yourself and finally be free of the past that has chained you for so long. There's a continued progression of going from the feeling of powerlessness, which is where we all start to a sense of purpose and personal power. As you go through chapter-by-chapter, that is the journey we'll be taking together, so pace yourself and start expecting the new, bolder and empowered you to emerge.

The big promise

The promise from me to you is that if you choose to walk this journey of healing with me and consume and implement all that I am sharing, you will heal and transform your life. You will be able to clearly identify, build a support system, and learn how to strengthen and protect yourself.

As I said before, my journey hasn't been easy, and it took me years to realize the real reasons behind the poor quality of life I was living. Once I realized that I was a victim, I made it my mission to make a change. I decided it must end with me.

My hope for you is that you will experience the same transformation and finally step into a greater experience of life, relationships, and love. I know it's not easy, but if you commit to taking this journey, you will come out victorious. Trust in the process and be willing to receive the new so that the old reality can become obsolete. If you're ready to begin the journey of self-healing, turn to the next chapter.

How to prepare to break free and heal from narcissistic abuse.

Depending on where you gather your information, you'll hear some people say healing takes just a few minutes while others say it will take at least a decade.

How long does it actually take to heal and recover from narcissistic abuse?
I don't have a definitive answer for you.

But wait, isn't this about healing and narcissistic abuse recovery?

Absolutely. That remains our main objective throughout this book, but sadly, what most people want is a magical silver bullet that will solve everything, and unfortunately, that doesn't exist.

The truth is, healing is a very personal thing. It is a journey, and each person will experience his or her recovery and restoration uniquely. While I cannot tell you exactly how long it will take to heal your specific situation, I can offer you six essential steps that will set a foundation for healing and help you step into this journey fully prepared to win. Failure to prepare yourself and lay down this foundation will lead to a lengthy process and might even cause you to fall off the wagon. To ensure you don't self-sabotage your own healing, do these five things:

1. Responsibility.
This is perhaps one of the most important things you will ever do in your life. Search through the rubble of your past, gather up what you need or want to keep and own it. Then tend to your wounds and find healthy ways to soothe yourself into full recovery. You are the victim of narcissistic abuse, but the only way to free yourself from that reality is to take full responsibility for your life and step out of victim mentality. You need to step up and become the King or Queen of your kingdom (so to speak) instead of allowing someone else to sit on the throne. Through this process of taking personal responsibility for how you feel, what you allow into your life and what you accept as true for you, it'll become easier to set healthy boundaries because you'll know exactly where to draw the line.

You will determine what treatment or behavior from another is acceptable to you and what you won't tolerate. At some point during your recovery, you'll see why boundaries and personal responsibility are imperative. It will start becoming evident to you that if you'd had these boundaries earlier on, or if you had begun taking full responsibility for your life earlier on, that last relationship with your ex wouldn't have landed you in another toxic experience. Your boundaries would have bounced that ex right out of your life, and it wouldn't have taken much effort from you. The web of lies, manipulation, and gaslighting wouldn't have worked on you as well, and you'd have spotted the repeat of this cycle long before it hurt you.

So what I want you to do now is to decide what boundaries you want to start implementing in your life. I also want you to make a decision that you are the sole owner of your life and that no one is responsible for your happiness, wellbeing, or success in life. Let your personal boundaries be an expression and extension of who you really believe you are. Define them and let them help you find your way back to the real and powerful you.

2. Commitment.
Make a commitment to yourself that you will no longer avoid or shy away from facing things as they are and making them better for yourself. The brain and body like to play all kinds of tricks on us, especially when we are leaving a dysfunctional relationship. As crazy as it sounds, victims tend to cling on to the very source of their trauma, especially when they believe it will take too long to heal or that it's too painful. This is referred to as a trauma bond (a bond usually established within the relationship as well as a biochemical addiction that forms in this environment).

Looking back at the early phases of your relationship where you were love bombed makes committing to this new life really hard for your brain to process because, on the one hand, you feel good thinking about this person. But deep down, you also know the heartache and pain they cause.

Commit that you are going to move forward and never look back; otherwise, you'll never fully recover and gain freedom from the abuse.

3. Acceptance.

Self-acceptance, acceptance of the fact that you will never be able to change or fix another person is crucial. I have met victims of narcissistic abuse who were seeking information about narcissists to try and "fix" their spouse or parent. This is all in vain.

For example, Kyle came into our healing community and said she was separated from her husband and business partner, but she was hoping to find a way to heal their marriage and help him heal his tortured soul. In her mind, the best way to save her marriage and keep her son happy was to focus on fixing the narcissistic. This is the wrong approach, and I trust that at this point, you're past this.

Accept that everyone needs to take personal responsibility for his or her life and actions. You might be the most loving, caring, kind, and wonderful partner in the world; it's still not your job to force someone to be what they aren't willing to be. Accept that you're in an unhealthy relationship, work on healing yourself, and move on.

4. Expectations.

Set realistic expectations of your recovery and the amount of time needed to heal fully. Setting wildly unrealistic recovery goals for yourself, hoping that a few meditations or a few therapy sessions will bring about quick healing is self-sabotage. Why? Because when that doesn't happen, you'll feel like a failure and create an opening for the old patterns to set in again. Like any transformation, healing is a journey of incremental success. That isn't to say you can't have a radical transformation where you suddenly recover. Perhaps it might happen for you, but get into it with a long-term view and if the miracle happens, all the better for you.

5. Understanding.

The more you can understand yourself, how the narcissist works, and how life works in general, the smoother this journey will become. I see so many aspiring survivors mistakenly believe that healing is merely getting out of the abusive relationship. Worse still, they believe reading a book, joining a forum or buying a course is enough to fix their situation. Unfortunately, this belief can keep you stuck for years if you're not careful because even if you physically leave the abusive relationship, healing requires more than just the physical act. Symptoms of trauma, depression, panic, complex grieve and anxiety are widespread among victims and aspiring survivors because they lack true understanding.

Don't get me wrong, reading, watching videos, joining a forum can be helpful, but they will not heal you. You will acquire knowledge and receive validation, but ultimately, the healing can only happen within. Your actions, the state of mind you place yourself in and the inner work you do are what will get you the results you desire.

Remember, our old mental, and emotional conditioning, trapped emotions, trauma, and patterns of thought determine our wellbeing. To truly heal, we must actively work on ourselves and gain true understanding about who we are, what our potential is, and where our real power lies.

6. Let go.
One of the hardest parts of ending any relationship is learning to let go, release, forgive, and detach. We talk more about this throughout the book, and I even help you practice the art of detachment. This is an inner shift and requires you to consciously recognize that you can make it alone; that you don't need to be defined by the narcissist or your relationship. It's about dissolving the belief that you need him or her to feel good about yourself or to be important in this world. I want you to slowly start training yourself to believe that no matter what you will be okay. It's a deep knowing that must be cultivated, and the nurturing of this knowing begins when you learn to stop attaching your identity, self-worth, and value to anything or anyone. Release the need to prove the narcissist wrong. Let go of waiting for apologies or closure and create a space for true healing within yourself that takes power off everything and everyone in your world and hands it over to you.

With these simple foundational steps, you are well on your way to true healing. But remember you must work through all five, in whatever order you prefer. To have the life of your dreams where true love, passion, freedom, and empowerment is a daily reality; you must set up a right and robust foundation.

"To live in this world, you must be able to do three things: Love what is mortal; hold it against your bones knowing your own life depends on it; and when the time comes to let it go, let it go."
- Mary Oliver.

Chapter 02: Recognizing The Abusive Narcissist

I think we can all agree that narcissism is created over a long and complicated psychological development that usually begins during childhood. While many people assume being selfish, arrogant, and attention seeking makes one a narcissist, the truth is they are not one and the same.

The great American psychologist William James believed that phenomena are best understood when placed within their series, studied in their germ and in their over-ripe decay". In the 2018 Cognitive Neuroscience of Narcissism J Brain Behav Cogn Sci Vol 1:6, I found a very enlightening resource that can help all of us better understand narcissism based off the same premise presented by William James. "If we take the phenomena of self-interest and observe it in its most germinal form, we see a Darwinian instinct that has great survival value. Moving up the series, a more severe form of self-interest, known as selfishness produces excessive or exclusive concern with oneself. The narcissistic needs to maintain a relatively positive self-image underlies individuals' needs for validation and affirmation as well as the motivation to overtly and covertly seek out validation and self-enhancement experiences from the social environment. This need can produce selfish behaviors such as cheating and lying, which undermine the efforts of organized society. However, selfishness is not considered pathological. Self-interest reaches its 'over-ripe decay' at the point of a narcissistic personality disorder (NPD) which depicts a pathological complex that is self-reinforcing and produces harmful effects on the individual, close relationships and possibly the broader social community." (George FR, Short D 2018 The Cognitive Neuroscience of Narcissism. J Brain Behav Cogn Sci Vol 1:6)

In other words, being a narcissist, in general, isn't considered pathological. But he or she may gradually develop a disorder if the behavior is left unchecked and carried to great extremity. Narcissism is a continuum that stretches across a spectrum. It is essential to realize that not all narcissists are considered pathological by medical standards and some narcissistic qualities may actually be beneficial to have as you will learn later on, but it's still wise to educate yourself as much as possible about their general tendencies of narcissists and how to spot a malignant type.

Who or what is a narcissist?

A narcissist is a specific type of person considered to be the opposite of an empath. Dealing with a narcissist is never easy, and it's important you learn to recognize if you have one in your life so you can better protect yourself and handle those relationships appropriately. Failure to do so may actually result in unnecessary suffering and wounds that damage your quality of relationships and experience of love.

According to the American Psychological Association, personality disorders are stable maladaptive patterns of behavior that involve at least two of the following four areas: Cognitive (thought patterns), affective (emotional patterns), interpersonal (patterns of relating to others) and impulse-control-based.

There are various types of personality disorders, which create impairment in how people function in their lives. In the United States of America alone, it is reported that about ten percent of the population is affected by some form of personality disorder. But when it comes to narcissistic personality disorders, they believe that it's still very rare with about one percent of the population actually suffering from it. When it comes to recognizing narcissists in your life, understand that not everyone who has narcissistic traits can be diagnosed as having NPD. But just because it's not extreme enough to be diagnosed doesn't mean they can't harm you. Here's an abbreviated summary of the diagnostic criteria for NDP according to the latest Diagnostic and Statistical Manual of Mental Disorders (DSM-V).
• A belief that he or she is "special" and unique and can only be understood by or should associate with similar high-status people.
• A grandiose sense of self-importance.
• Highly manipulative.
• A need for excessive admiration.
• Monopolization of conversations to belittle or degrade the people they perceive as inferior.
• A tendency to use others for their own needs and wants.
• Unable to handle criticism of any kind.
• Lack of empathy and inability to recognize the needs and feelings of others.
• An exaggerated arrogance demonstrated in behavior and/ or attitude.
• Lack of remorse for hurting others and never experience guilt.

The narcissist's false self and true self:

We all have our "ego ideal" that helps us orient our goals and navigate life. When this ego ideal is pathologically distorted, it becomes the false self. In general, we all create a mental representation of the ideal state of the self, which usually possesses every perfection. In the case of narcissism, this becomes even more evident.

The underlying factors that lead to extreme personality disorder, which are frequently wounds that require healing get suppressed and layered up with a false image. This false image is the one the narcissist initially presents to you, and because they are so good at facades, it takes a while before you can start to see cracks in the mask. Because the narcissist is doing everything they can to avoid dealing with his or her unresolved wounds, they strive to find distractions and energy sources that can help them attain an ideal that they believe the real (and hidden) self is incapable of achieving. In other words, they try to live purely from the ego self and make it as powerful as possible.

To solicit attention, admiration, and get the supply he or she needs, a narcissist will flaunt a false self. He or she pretends to be all-powerful, omnipotent, unique, brilliant, and superior to you. It's good to remember that the false self in malignant narcissists is an adaptive reaction to pathological circumstances, but its dynamics make it predominant. The false self in the narcissist devours the psyche and preys upon the true self (and the inner child) of the individual. This is why such people are unable to express and portray a healthy, flexible, and holistically functioning personality.

The remnants of an authentic self are usually so shredded and repressed into submission that for all practical purposes this true self in the narcissist is rendered dysfunctional. In a malignant narcissist, the false self completely takes over and imitates the true self causing the narcissist to reinterpret certain negative emotions and reactions in a flattering socially acceptable light. For example, instead of admitting fear, the narcissist will usually try to justify how they feel in a way that solicits admiration or compassion. Malignant narcissists also emulate and fake things like compassion, empathy, affection, and so on to prey on their victims so they can create a stable source of supply that can feed the false self.

The narcissist's ego-self, which is always power hungry, can invest in physical objects or oneself to reclaim this desired ideal while muting out healthy emotional investments to reclaim that missing sense of wholeness. The possession of material objects seems to help increase self-confidence and self-esteem in the narcissist. The same thing also happens when it comes to places and people that the narcissist considers valuable. Their own sense of value and self-worth increases when they associate with such people, and as such, they go to great lengths to only associate with organizations, people, and places they consider superior.

A narcissist will only pay attention to you when he or she feels like you help them get closer to their ego ideal so whenever there's a discrepancy in your interaction with them, only negativity can result because they will feel wounded and resentful.

For example, think of a time when the narcissist in your life gave you a strange look as though you had done something wrong simply because of how intelligently you answered a question or how skillfully you executed an action. That was probably one of the first red flags that you chose to ignore because you wanted to maintain peace or because the person had been so charming otherwise. Jealousy and envy is something a narcissist will struggle with a lot because they always want to be the ones winning and performing things that others marvel at.

To a narcissist's mind, you are undermining them when you do something wonderful because your role should be something that helps them shine, not the other way around. At the start of the relationship; however, what you experience is the false mask covering the wounded ego self that they are trying to build up. The charm, thoughtfulness, attentiveness, loving, caring nature is just a facade meant to entice you into their vortex of narcissistic abuse. As long as you're the distraction that's keeping them in the calm zone, it won't be easy to unmask their ego self, and it will undoubtedly feel impossible to understand what their true self is like.

If as you go through this description, there's resonance within you, then it's probably a good thing you're here because it is time to sever the bond you have with this person. Their problematic behavior and the difficulty you have in dealing with them is good enough cause to distance yourself from such relationships. Narcissists are generally happy, far happier at least than the people in their lives because they aren't aware (or don't care) about the negative consequences of their behavior and actions. So it's highly unlikely a narcissist will agree to therapy, which can include a diagnosis.

Most people seek therapy out of discomfort and pain, which isn't usually something the narcissist will be dealing with. Although it is unethical for a trained therapist to diagnose friends and family with NPD due to potential bias and certainly not an official diagnosis for you as a layperson to view the diagnostic criteria and declare someone to have a psychological disorder, I do encourage you to educate yourself thoroughly. Get to understand the signs, observe your current situations, and the state of the relationships that bring you pain and suffering. Empower yourself with knowledge and then do something to improve your life.

Don't mind too much about forcing a narcissist to get help once you recognize you're in a relationship with one. Instead, work on your self-healing and building a new lifestyle that frees you from that relationship.

In the next chapter we will be diving deeper into the different types of narcissists you need to become aware of and some of the traits they possess but before then, let's shed some light on what narcissistic abuse is and some of the ways it may present itself.

What is narcissistic abuse?

Narcissistic abuse is a term coined by Sam Vaknin that refers to any kind of abuse by a narcissist. Typically emotional abuse, it often occurs in adult-adult relationships or parent-child relationships.

To fully comprehend what narcissistic abuse is we need to view it as a spectrum with varying degrees. It stretches from ignoring your feelings to violent outbursts of rage, aggression, and everything in between.

Few narcissists will self-reflect and even feel guilty of their actions when they mistreat you so as a general rule, don't expect them to take responsibility for their behavior. According to some studies, an adult who experiences a relationship with a narcissist will tend to struggle with knowing what true love (or a healthy relationship) is. There's also a tendency for children who grow up with narcissists to become victims of narcissistic abuse in their adult years.

Different types of abuse to become aware of:

- Verbal abuse - this includes shaming, criticizing, sarcasm, bullying, threatening, undermining, interrupting, and name-calling.
- Manipulation - this of usually an expression of covert aggression.
- Negative contrasting - this is often when the narcissist is unnecessarily comparing you with others in a negative way.
- Lying - this involves persistent deception to avoid responsibility or to achieve the narcissist's own needs.
- Neglect - this consists of ignoring the needs of a partner or a child. In the case of narcissistic parents, it includes child endangerment such as leaving a child in dangerous situations.
- Sabotage - this involves disruptive interference with your endeavors for personal advantage or for revenge.
- Withholding - this includes keeping things such as money, sex, or affection from you.

Can empaths be narcissists too?

The first time I asked this question in my online community for healing survivors, I was met with a lot of resistance. I mean empaths are supposed to be the opposites of narcissists, right?

Well, here's the thing. Being an empath doesn't automatically mean you always feel empathy toward others, and being a narcissist doesn't mean you are utterly incapable of feeling what others feel.

We tend to make it a black and white scenario, which isn't exactly right. Most of us only perceive narcissists as obnoxious extroverted self-obsessed people. Think most Hollywood celebrities.

But did you know there are overt and covert narcissists?

Overt narcissists are habitually thick-skinned and openly conceited.
Covert narcissists are usually shy, sensitive, and introverted. It's crucial you learn to recognize the signs and traits as both types possess similar characteristics, but of course, the covert will be way harder to spot. In fact, many times, they may mask themselves as empaths.

I have a friend who finally confessed to this discovery in his own life. For years he firmly believed that he was an empath. He created an idealized self-image that masked the fact that underneath he was actually a wounded, self-centered egomaniac who couldn't truly empathize. He tended to shift from acting superior to others and feeling hurt by them. He always felt victimized by life and other people.

One of the key insights he discovered while going through the self-healing journey was that within him was the darkness that was being masked by his empathic self-image. His sensitive, vulnerable, and introverted nature did not cancel out his narcissistic tendencies. For years he struggled with this feeling that he was a victim of everyone else's feelings and thoughts. And even though he felt other people's pain so strongly, he had little understanding toward them.

What this taught me is that even with empaths, it is possible to have underlying wounds that need healing. One becomes a narcissistic empath when he or she denies or avoids the feeling of vulnerability that comes with that level of sensitivity, and of course, this stems from having low self-esteem. Narcissistic empaths are too concerned about protecting themselves that they shut out their ability to genuinely care for others.
This question "can empaths be narcissists" cannot have a straight yes or no answer. It's obviously up for considerable debate, and I'm sure you'll have your opinion as well, but I encourage you to keep an open mind and be on the lookout for certain common symptoms that non-regular narcissists would tend to demonstrate. Here are a few:
• Feeling fundamentally different from others and more unique.
• Perceiving others in extremes and being overly judgmental. For example, demonizing a person.
• Self-martyrdom as a way of manipulating and controlling others.

- Finger pointing and a tendency to blame others instead of taking responsibility for their actions and feelings.
- Intensely offended by any sign of criticism.

Chapter 03: What You May Not Know About Narcissism and NPD

First of all, let's break an old myth that usually confuses a lot of people. Narcissism is not all negative. There is a difference between healthy narcissism and narcissistic abuse. According to psychologist Dr. Susan Kolod, everyone needs to practice a good dose of healthy narcissism. The diagnosis of narcissistic personality disorder is indeed very negative and includes characteristics such as arrogance, preoccupation with oneself, a need for constant admiration and most importantly, a lack of empathy for others. But narcissism itself is not positive or negative - there is a continuum from healthy to pathological, Kolod says.

According to Dr. Kolod, healthy narcissism is related to self-esteem and self-worth, and it involves being able to take pleasure in one's beauty and experiencing ecstatic joy in oneself.

Why is having healthy narcissism necessary?

Well, if you can experience joy in yourself, feel proud of your accomplishment and feel worthy, then you can face many difficult challenges boldly. It can also help you experience a sense of self-satisfaction and fulfillment in your own work and the impact you have on the world. When children aren't raised in an environment that helps them develop healthy narcissism, that's when things start going wrong.
On the other hand, when one suffers from a narcissistic personality disorder, they fall into the extreme of these tendencies and develop inflated self-importance and an excessive need for attention and admiration.

The Cause Of Narcissism

As mentioned above, narcissistic tendencies are quite normal for most human beings. Think of a 2-year-old baby who is in love with the world and has just discovered "mine" and "I." The child will naturally demonstrate tendencies of narcissism and then slowly grow into an understanding that relating to others requires a shift (assuming the parents do a good job teaching this). If however, the child grows up in a dysfunctional family, then what would be a healthy sense of narcissism will likely And then we get the extreme version that often leads to narcissistic abuse. This is usually what's medically diagnosed as a personality disorder, and the root cause of all the pain, hurt, and suffering victims of narcissistic abuse have to endure. Going back to the statement offered by William James that implies every phenomenon has a point of becoming over-ripe, this point is reached when narcissistic tendencies are taken to an extreme and turn into a personality disorder. Although we cannot state with certainty what causes this, we do know three major factors act as a catalyst.

• Psychological or environmental factors

This, to me, seems to be one of the main factors that lead to NPD. It could be early childhood trauma, heartbreak, mid-life crisis, or grief. Children who lacked proper parental support and care or those shuffled between foster parents are more prone to this disorder because they usually suffer from an identity crisis.

• Biological factors

Malignant narcissism can literally be passed down from one generation to the next within a family. But we cannot attribute causation to genes alone. If narcissistic parents raised a man, and he develops similar traits, there are there biological factors that can turn him into a malignant narcissist.

First and foremost, his temperament. If he lacks emotional control and maturity and is considered quick-tempered, extravagant, attention seeking, and self-indulgent, then he can quickly develop NPD.

Second would be his neurobiology. If certain changes occur in this neurobiological system, it might influence his judgment, social skills, problem-solving skills, and the way he responds to stress in general.

Third would be a genetic influence because even though we know genes cannot be the sole reason for developing NPD, we cannot overrule its influence. According to recent research on genetics, scientists have discovered that if one monozygotic twin has a criminal background, then there's a 66% chance the other might also exhibit the same behavior, but the numbers significantly reduce to 31% chance if they are dizygotic twins.

• Social and cultural factors

Cultural confusion, unemployment, migration, media can all contribute to this disorder for a narcissist who struggles to regulate his or her emotions. Usually, malignant narcissism comes along with other psychiatric disorders such as depression, borderline, and antisocial personality disorders.

Bottom line is, malignant narcissists can be very harmful and create a lot of damage in your life if you continue hanging around them, so you need to know how to face them and escape that pit of despair and suffering.

What is NPD?

A narcissistic personality disorder is a diagnosed medical condition that turns narcissists into unhealthy, dangerous people, especially on a mental and emotional level. These people are exploitative, entitled, and lack empathy. They are so addicted to feeling special that they'll use extreme measures including stealing, cheating, sabotage, lying, or whatever else it takes to get what they want. And they have no concern or compassion for those they affect in the process.

As with all personality disorders, the exact nature of narcissistic personality disorder (NPD) cannot be drilled down to a single event. It's usually a combination of early childhood experiences, psychological factors, and sometimes even genes.

Early childhood factors include trauma, abuse, excessive criticism, extremely high expectations, and intensive parenting. It could also be a result of being hypersensitive (as in the case of empaths) and not knowing how to handle the sensitivities very well. Although the single root cause remains unknown, all professionals agree that getting treatment is vital. The sooner the treatment is given, the higher the chances of lessening or even wholly healing from the disorder.

The less commonly discussed problem is the wake of devastation that a narcissist leaves behind as they interact with people. Some cases are so server they can affect the entire future of the victim. Here's a story that a friend shared, which helps show how awful life can be for those of us subjected to narcissistic abuse.

Sarah survived decades of emotional abuse from her mother. She said everything was always blamed on her. The mother would often say, "you should have been aborted, you're poison." As she got older, her narcissistic mother started sexually shaming her by repeatedly telling her no boys would ever find her attractive because she had no breasts. Sarah said that her mother was like a vampire finding any excuse to feed on Sarah's pain and anguish. It's easy to see why the girl grew up with no self-esteem, always afraid to speak her mind or state her desires. At the age of 18, she went for an interview hoping to be hired as a tutor but the woman interviewing her was so alarmed at how insecure, jittery and shy Sarah was that she kept asking her if everything was okay.

Sarah didn't get that job, and it took a lot of work to finally get her out of that state of insecurity and feeling invisible. She confessed that she felt as though she was nothing, invaluable in the world and that she didn't feel like she had a real identity to present to the world.

Another excellent example of how narcissistic abuse presents itself in adult-to-adult relationships can be seen in Gemma's story. Gemma Matheson met Alex at a party of a Friday night having been introduced by mutual friends. They spent all evening flirting, dancing, drinking, and having a blast. By Saturday afternoon the next day, the two were a couple. Alex was a charming Real Estate agent with his sights on the top position at his company. He even had a four-year plan laid out for how he would get it. " We met Friday night, and by the following weekend, he was taking mortgages, a big wedding, and kids," says Gemma. She completely fell for him believing that finally, she had found Mr. Right. The perfect man who was in it for the long haul. Six months into the relationship and his euphoric highs and romantic gestures were countered by severe aloofness and painful rejection. "He'd invite me to dinner or a party, then cancel the offer minutes before we were due to go out and once he actually canceled a holiday hours before our flight. I thought nothing of it and soon became standard behavior because I always made allowances for these types of behaviors. Looking back, I should have known how it would all end." laments Gemma.

In spring of last year, Alex said he was planning a special surprise dinner during which time he proposed to Gemma who obviously said yes. Three days after the special dinner, Alex sent a text message terminating their relationship, and Gemma hasn't heard from him since. The mutual friend that introduced them was just as shocked and said Alex seems to be doing well but avoids talking about what happened. Each time it comes up, he simply says that he's working out some stuff and would rather not discuss it. This is a classic symptom of avoidant personality disorder combined with narcissism, and unfortunately, Gemma is left to pick up the pieces of her broken heart.

These are just a few of the countless stories that we'll often hear in our community of people who are trying to get out of or recover from narcissistic abuse. The term best used to describe those of us that suffer the consequences of narcissism is Echoism. It was first coined in a 2005 paper by psychoanalyst Dean Davis and popularized by psychologist Dr. Craig Malkin Ph.D. who wrote a book called Rethinking Narcissism.

What is echoism, and what does it have to do with narcissistic abuse?

Echoism is a trait that Dr. Malkin and his colleagues are currently studying and it's starting to gain a lot of attention, especially with survivors of narcissistic abuse. According to his research, Dr. Malkin believes it is a trait that exists in all of us. For some, it is stronger and more pronounced while in others, it's very subtle. Dr. Malkin says that people who score above average in echoism qualify as echoists and their defining characteristic is a fear of being a burden or coming across as narcissistic. Most of these people are warm-hearted and kind, but they feel uncomfortable about receiving praise and attention.

In other words, echoists, especially those who are extremely abundant with this trait, never feel special, and they suffer greatly for it. Because they don't want to be a burden or to shine, they are naturally attracted to narcissists who have no trouble grabbing the spotlight overshadowing the emotional anxiety experienced by an echoist.

Echoism arises when someone is in a toxic relationship with a narcissist.
This concept of echoism is drawn from the Greek myth of Narcissus and Echo. Narcissus is the god who became entranced by his own reflection. A familiar tale many of us have heard. What we don't usually hear is the story of Echo, the wood nymph who was cursed to near-silence and able only to repeat the last words she hears.

Echo fell in love with Narcissus, but all she could do was echo what he said. Just like Echo in Greek Mythology, echoists tend to fall into relationships with narcissists because they struggle to have a voice of their own. They become proficient at echoing the needs of the narcissist in their lives and ultimately lose their identity and self-worth. Victims of narcissistic abuse learn to bury their needs, feelings, and preferences and develop coping mechanisms to survive the relationship.

Dr. Malkin shares a very vulnerable story that helps us understand how he came up with this concept during the writing of his famous book "Rethinking Narcissism."
"As a child, I struggled to celebrate my achievements. I found reasons to dismiss praise with statements such as - the test was easy, or the teacher likes me. And I blamed myself whenever someone hurt me. I was far more comfortable providing care than receiving it. It was only many years later when I was writing Rethinking Narcissism and rereading the myth or Narcissus that I had an aha moment. Like the love-struck nymph in the myth, echoists, like myself, can echo the needs and feelings of others, but we are at a loss when it comes to 'voicing' our own desires. We play Echo to Narcissus, shrinking from the special attention that narcissists thrive on."

It's important to note here that Dr. Malkin considers echoism a trait, not a disorder and at best should be thought of as a survival strategy for those who struggle to enjoy the feeling of being special and important.

Eventually, the victims and survivors of narcissistic abuse will seek out therapy because they feel depressed, suffer from anxiety or feel like they are on the verge of going crazy even if they don't know why they feel that way. If you're reading this and recognizing your own story of abuse, know that it's not your fault and you are not alone. Help is available, and you can heal yourself from that life of devastation. The more aware you become of narcissistic behavior and traits that you possess that make you an easy target, the easier it will to spot and avoid them on your road to recovery.

There are many free websites online that offer quizzes to help you determine whether you or someone you know is exhibiting symptoms of either mild or a more severe case of narcissistic personality disorder. I encourage you to take the quiz but with the bearing in mind that it does not medically diagnose NPD.

Different types of narcissists

From a medical standpoint, there is only one diagnosis for narcissistic disorders, but within it are multiple variants and degrees of severity.
According to a 2012 review of the research on narcissism, some of these variants that were identified included grandiose narcissists, vulnerable narcissists, and malignant narcissists.

Grandiose narcissists require excessive praise and attention. Vulnerable narcissists tend to have a lot of anxiety issues and need lots of supportive attention.

Malignant narcissists are considered the most damaging of them all because beyond being overly self-focused, they tend to have a darker side to their self-absorption. This subset tends to have antisocial traits and even a sadistic streak. In fact, some experts see little difference between psychopaths and malignant narcissists because they both have a sadistic, antisocial streak with almost no empathy for others.

Our primary focus in this book is on malignant narcissists because they are the more common and most damaging types when it comes to our interaction with them. Other types may be less dangerous but certainly equally annoying and challenging to be around, but as it relates to your well-being and narcissistic abuse, malignant narcissists are definitely the ones you must become wary of.

What are some traits and symptoms of a narcissist?

It's only fair that I share with you some new research that shows there are some positive and beneficial traits that a narcissist has that could help him or her succeed in life. Researchers at Queen's University Belfast have found that narcissists possess what the researchers have dubbed as "mental toughness." An ability that propels them into success.

As much as narcissism is considered negative, some doctors are starting to believe that's it's not all bad. A lecturer at the school of psychology by the name of Dr. Kostas Papageorgiou did a study called Mental Toughness: A Personality Trait That Is Relevant Across Achievement And Mental Health Outcomes. In the study, he discovered that adolescents who display some of the traits associated with narcissism might also be more mentally tough, and because of this perform better at school. As part of the study, three hundred and forty students were recruited from three different high schools in Milan, and researchers looked to see if there was an association between mental toughness and achievement. Their findings proved that mental toughness correlated with narcissism. Dr. Papageorgiou seems to think people with narcissistic traits could actually do more good than harm if they kept themselves in check at all times. "People who score high on subclinical narcissism may be at an advantage because their heightened sense of self-worth may mean they are more motivated assertive and successful in certain contexts," said Dr. Papageorgiou.

So there's probably some positivity to being a narcissist but usually not for those around such a person. Often it is their initial positive aspect that attracts us, especially in intimate relationships. That's why before we talk about the negative traits of a malignant narcissist; I want to make you aware of some of the positive characteristics narcissists have that usually draw innocent victims into their web of devastation.

- Charismatic.
- Witty.
- Romantic.
- Ambitious.
- Attentive and affection, especially in the early stages.
- Very confident and high self-esteem.
- Persuasiveness.

Personality disorders, especially malignant narcissism, carries certain traits that are relatively easy to spot. Here are some signs to look out for:

- A heightened sense of entitlement.

A malignant narcissist always has unreasonable expectations of superior treatment. They feel entitled to have what they want when they want, as they want it, and people should automatically comply with their demands. The narcissist's world is very black and white. It's good/bad, right/wrong, superior/inferior, and he or she is always on the right side of things. Narcissists have to win all the time no matter what, and they must be the best at everything.

- Grandiosity.

Malignant narcissists, in general, believe they are superior to most people and are better than most people. A malignant narcissist takes this sense to a whole new level and actually lashes out when people don't adapt to this worldview. They believe "I am everything and you are nothing; I have everything, and you have nothing." Anyone who contradicts that viewpoint stands to suffer much, especially if the narcissists perceive the person as inferior to them.

- Egocentricity.

Narcissists have egos that are totally out of control. He or she only talks about himself or herself and continually seeks praise and compliments. In truth, they believe the world revolves around them, and everyone is there to serve their needs. The danger of being around an egocentric narcissist is that you stand to be on the receiving end of their rage if you choose to contradict their perspective or want to disagree with the way they do things.

- Perfectionism.

This is very common for most narcissists because they have an extreme need for everything to be perfect. They want to control each and every detail around them to make sure it matches the high standards they've set for themselves, and when that fails to happen, things become really bad for those around them. According to a narcissist, life should play out exactly as they envision it.

- Lack of boundaries.

A narcissistic cannot see where they end and you begin, which means as far as they are concerned, everything belongs to them, and everyone thinks, feels, and wants the same things they want. Think of a 2-year-old's behavior, and you're pretty close to understanding how a narcissist operates. If a narcissist wants something from you, he or she will go to any lengths to get it whether the means used are healthy or harmful.

- Manipulation.

It's not uncommon for all of us to try to use a situation to our advantage at times, but true manipulation runs deeper than the occasional cajoling. Real narcissists are experts at constant manipulation. They are not interested in the well-being of others and only cares about people when they can see how to use them as a vehicle to gain control, power, or profit in some way. Narcissists are so good at manipulation that they can take what you say or do and twist it around so much to the point where you start to question your own truth and reality.

- Deceitfulness.

Narcissists are usually very deceitful and regularly lie, con people, cheat and malinger just to get personal profit or pleasure. Their inability to "put themselves in another person's shoes" makes it easy for them to lie without any guilty conscience. The most important thing for them is that they come out looking good and in possession of what they desire. Sometimes they will use rationalization to twist words in their favor, which can make it difficult for the victim to figure out what is real and what is false about the narcissist's behavior.

- Lack of empathy.

Narcissists are unable to feel and empathize with the experience of another. They cannot process emotions the same we the rest of us do, which also means they usually don't experience the same sensation of guilt or remorse an average person would if they acted poorly. Due to the fact that narcissists cannot comprehend what other people are feeling, it's hard for them to see their actions as wrong and in fact, many believe that they are the victims of criticism and mistreatment.

- Sadistic and cruel.

Narcissists, especially malignant narcissists, tend to enjoy inflicting pain. They possess this sadistic quality that promotes taking advantage of people, inflicting harm, and humiliation.

- Inexplicable Hatred and anger.

Most malignant narcissists carry a lot of rage and anger without reason, and those around them tend to be on the receiving end of these negative emotions, which creates emotional abuse. When exposed to such a person as a child or adult, it's easy to blame yourself and internalize the rage and hatred you experience, which becomes very damaging. But there is never a logical reason, and it's not your fault when the narcissists act out in this way.

- Paranoia.

Although many people experience some level of paranoia, it doesn't occur as often or as intensely as it does with a malignant narcissist. He or she will over analyze everything people say and approach all people with suspicion and criticism even though they don't like to receive any form of criticism. For example, if someone happens to bump into a malignant narcissist at the bar, the narcissists will view this as something intentionally done to cause them harm in some way even if it was just a pure accident. They are especially paranoid that other people may be trying to take away their power, possessions, or harm them in some twisted way.

- Projection.

This usually happens when the narcissist projects their behavior onto someone else mostly because they are unwilling to see their own shortcomings. The malignant narcissists may know of his or her shortcomings but rather than admit them, they prefer to deflect and insist that the rest of the world is guilty of doing what they are doing. This is why you'll find many malignant narcissists claiming that they are the victims being mistreated and so the real victims of narcissistic abuse end up feeling like everything is their fault.

- Fear.

A narcissist is strongly motivated by fear, but much of the time, these fears are deeply buried and repressed, making it hard to spot them. The main reason narcissists cannot take any criticism, rejection, or ridicule is because of this deeply hidden fear. If you're observant, you can see this fear surfacing, especially when the narcissist feels threatens or if they believe someone is out to get their power, status, money, etc. Most narcissists fear being vulnerable or having real intimacy with anyone because they are afraid you will see their inadequacies and imperfections and judge or reject them.

I have realized its almost impossible for narcissists to develop real trust and love of others because the deep-seated fear controlling their lives is always in control, so they do everything possible to mask it because they don't want to be found out or abandoned by the people around them.

This is list is far from exhausted, and with a little more research I'm sure you'll find lots more signs and symptoms that can help you understand whether you're dealing with a malignant narcissist or not. Aside from the symptoms, there are also varying levels of narcissism you must become aware of.

Types of extreme narcissists

Narcissism occurs along a continuum of expression that ranges from healthy to unhealthy, as I mentioned in an earlier chapter. Here are a few types you might easily encounter in our modern society.

- The bullying narcissist

This type of person builds himself or herself by humiliating other people. The example I shared about Sarah and her mother is a perfect example of a bullying narcissist, and such a person tends to be very brutal about the way they assert their superiority.

He or she will belittle and mock you, make you feel like you are nothing, and have no value. Such a person makes you doubt yourself and your value as a human being.

- The seductive narcissist

Unlike many of the extreme narcissists, this type of person actually manipulates you by making you feel good about yourself. At first, he or she idolizes and offers lots of admiration, but the ultimate goal is to use you in some way. Such a person craves support and admiration and will use flattery and seduction to get it, but when they get to a point where they have no further use for you, all you'll get is a cold shoulder.

- The Vindictive Narcissist

This type of narcissism can be very damaging to your life. He or she is very much into revenge and getting back at you. At work, they might try to get you fired, or if it's an ex-wife, she might do everything in her power to turn the kids against you. Such a person knows no limits when it comes to getting back at people they believe have wronged them in some way.

- The grandiose narcissist

This type of person is quite common in today's world. We can easily recognize him or her. Such a person believes they are more important, influential, and superior than others. They love showing off their accomplishments and always exaggerate their importance in an attempt to gain more admiration or make others envious. This type of narcissist truly believes they are destined for great things and as a matter of fact, can accomplish a lot and succeed in the business world due to their overgrown ambitions.

- The know-it-all

This type of narcissists is the one we all found annoying in school. Always eager to give their opinion even when no one asked and believes they know everything. He or she likes to argue, lecture, and condescending people and struggles to listen because they are always so self-absorbed. Instead of genuinely listening to you, they would be busy thinking about what they'd like to say next. Although not as damaging as the previously mentioned types, it's still good to be on the lookout and to avoid these types of people.

Traits of perfect targets for narcissists

Some people find themselves in a narcissistic relationship, break their way out, and spend the rest of their lives avoiding narcissists. Then there are those of us who just seem to be magnets for narcissists.
We dig ourselves out of one relationship with a narcissist only to find ourselves trapped in a new one.

A friend of mine spent years clawing her way out of narcissistic abuse with her dad, and a few years later, she was in a new abusive situation. Regardless of which one hits close to home for you know that there is nothing wrong with you. There is, however, an active tendency in you to attract narcissists, perhaps due to certain qualities you possess, and it's imperative you increase your awareness.

Certain personality types and characteristics are very appealing to narcissists, and it's crucial you get to learn more about yourself so you can see why they seem to "prey" on you or why you have a tendency of falling victim to a narcissist.

Narcissists, especially those that are malignant are good at carefully choosing, charming, seducing, and trapping a victim. Your energy is then used to feed him or her. It's what gives the narcissist a foot in the door to carry out their manipulation tactics and devastate your life.

- You are highly sensitive to other people's feelings, and you love unconditionally.

Don't get me wrong here, this is one of your greatest strengths, and loving people unconditionally is supposed to be a wonderful thing in an ideal world. Unfortunately, when it comes to narcissists, this quality makes you a magnet for them because when he or she understands this about you and exploiting that gift will be the natural impulse.

You may have experienced moments where your abuser apologizes, starts crying or showers you with praise only to plunge you back into that feeling of worthlessness. They usually create this facade to make us believe that they love us and they use it to keep us hooked until the next outburst so don't fall for this trick anymore.

• You're always reliable, dependable, and ready to help others.

If you tend to keep a low profile and have no wish to overshadow the people in your life, then a narcissist sees this as a perfect opportunity to trap you in their web of lies.

• You have a natural desire to heal others

This applies a lot to empaths, which is probably why they are the biggest magnets for narcissists. If you feel everyone in the world needs to be loved and that given the right environment and attention anyone can change then you'll naturally feel attracted to a narcissist. Something in you will always want to heal and fix narcissists because you believe they can turn themselves around and stop hurting people. The narcissists will naturally feel attracted to you and will be more than happy to cling to you for dear life.

When a narcissist knows you will never turn down their fight and that you're emotionally attached to them, manipulating you for personal gain becomes the game to play and trust me; they enjoy the game of manipulation a lot.

• You're trusting and vulnerable to everyone.

If unlike most people, you naturally trust people and expect them to do the right thing and treat you with respect, then a narcissist will likely use this to their advantage. He or she knows it's easy to get away with lying and deceit because you never doubt their actions or motives. They also see your openness and vulnerability as a weakness to be exploited for personal gain.

Chapter 04: Tools of manipulation

Toxic people like malignant narcissists engage in maladaptive habits that ultimately exploit, hurt, and demean their family members, friends, and intimate relationships. They will usually use a variety of tactics that distort the reality of their victims and are really good at deflecting responsibility. Check to see if you've experienced any of these in the past or present within your relationships. And as soon as you recognize an active tactic in your life, apply the helpful suggestions provided.

1. Gaslighting

It is the most stealthy and manipulative tactic out there. When a narcissist gaslights you two conflicting beliefs battle it out: is this person right or do I trust what I experienced?
A manipulative narcissist will usually throw statements at you like "that didn't happen," "are you crazy?" or "you're imagining things." He or she will try to convince you that you can't trust your own ideas anymore.

Do this:
As soon as you become aware that someone in your life is gaslighting you, ground yourself in your own reality. Journal your thoughts or speak to a close friend so you can find the strength to resist this need to make yourself dysfunctional and the other person right. The more you can validate your own thoughts and reality, the easier it will be to trust your inner guidance rather than ideas coming from a person who always makes you feel wrong.

2. Avoiding accountability at all costs.

Narcissists usually use this tactic when they don't want to own up to something. He or she will literally change the actual topic and redirect attention to a different issue altogether. For example, if you start complaining to your narcissistic husband about their neglectful parenting, he might bring up the one mistake you committed even before the children were born. To spot this in your life, take note of when the person starts deviating from the topic at hand. Usually he or she will say something like "What about that time when you..."

Do this:
The next time someone tries to derail you, give him or her the chance to speak, listen, and gently (but firmly) bring him or her back to what you were saying. Act like a broken record and keep stating the facts without giving in to their tactic. If they are not interested, step back, preserve your energy, and move on to something more constructive.

3. Name-calling

Narcissists generally blow things out of proportion, especially when they feel threatened in any way. Narcissistic rage is very common, and as Mark Goulson, M.D says, narcissistic rage does not result from low self-esteem but rather a very high sense of entitlement and a false sense of superiority. Name-calling is one of the lowest forms of rage demonstrated by narcissists who want to degrade and insult your intelligence or appearance quickly. They also use it to criticize beliefs, opinions, and insights.

Do this:
End all interactions and communication once someone starts name-calling you. Let him, or her know you will not tolerate it and make sure you don't take things personally. Internalizing, it only gives them the joy they were seeking to begin with. Realize there is a hidden deficiency and insecurity that's driving them to act so lowly.

4. Covert and overt threats.

Malignant narcissists usually get very offended and threatened by anything that challenges their sense of entitlement, superiority, and grandiosity. They impose unrealistic demands on those around them, and when those needs aren't meant rather than deal healthily with conflict or try to find a compromise, they will usually resort to threats. Because they are always right and must always win, your perspective or feelings are never taken into consideration. This makes it impossible to ever truly satisfy a narcissist.

Do this:
Whenever someone threatens you in any way for having a different opinion or perspective, take it seriously and see it as a red flag. If you are already dealing with a narcissist that's threatening your well being in any way, start taking action. Document these threats and report them to the appropriate authority; don't wait till it's too late.

5. Projection.

This is another tactic commonly used by malignant narcissists because they are usually unwilling to see their own shortcomings. When dealing with such a person, he or she will do everything in their power to avoid being held accountable for their actions and especially their deficiencies. Projection is a defense mechanism used to deflect one's own negative behavior and attributing it to someone else. According to Narcissistic Personality Disorder clinical expert Dr. Martinez-Lewi, the projections of a narcissist are often psychologically abusive. Instead of acknowledging their own flaws, imperfections, and wrongdoings, malignant narcissists choose to dump their personal traits on their victims in ways that are usually very cruel and painful.

For example, if your partner often calls you "clingy" in an attempt to make you feel like you're the one who is dependent on them, then you're probably being manipulated using this tactic. Malignant narcissists love to shame others and play the blame shifting game. Usually, it's you and/or the world that is to blame for everything that's wrong with them. And your job as their victim is to nurse and babysit that fragile ego.

Do this:
Stop projecting your compassion and empathy on to such people and by all means, stop carrying the burden of their toxicity. Don't own any of their projections. You don't have to live in someone else's cesspool of dysfunction anymore, so cut off those ties and put an end to the blame game.

6. Love-bombing and devaluation.

Malignant narcissists at first seem very charming and attentive. They idealize you until you're hooked and emotionally invested in the relationship then they begin devaluing you. They are notorious for putting their intimate partners up on a pedestal at the start of the relationship and a few months in turn things around drastically. But this isn't the only tactic used. Sometimes the narcissist will put you on a pedestal and devalue their ex. Unfortunately, when the dust settles, you'll be on the same receiving end that same experience because the very thing they admire about you now might become the insults they throw around to devalue you.

Do this:
Be more mindful of how a person speaks or treats other people. Don't get too carried away with receiving over the top attention and praise, especially at the start of a relationship. It might end up clouding your judgment. Know that the way someone speaks and treats their previous partners is potentially the way you'll be treated in the future.

7. Triangulation.

This is a widespread trick between lovers. Malignant narcissists love to evoke jealousy and uncertainty by playing this card. They will use strangers, co-workers, ex-partners, friends, and even family members if they have to. It's a tactic used to distract you from the unhealthy, abusive behavior he or she may be exposing you to so you can have a false image of them. They want to appear desirable and can go to any lengths to show just how important they are and how "everybody wants to be with them." It usually works well to manufacture love triangles that often hurt the victims and leaves them feeling unhinged.

Do this:
Step back from the triangulation and increase your awareness. Recognize that everyone under the influence of the narcissist is mostly being played and that you are all victims of this sick game. Then decide who you want to be. Seek out your own validation and if necessary, gain support from someone outside the narcissist's circle of influence.

8. Aggressive blows disguised as jokes.

Covert narcissists enjoy taking pleasure at your expense so it shouldn't come as a surprise that humor is used to inject shame, humiliation, and pain into your experience. They are not "just jokes," and you're not paranoid or too stuck up. These people just want to get away with saying appalling things while still preserving their calm demeanor. This is one I have experienced a lot in my old relationship. Each time I would say something, my abuser would claim I have no sense of humor. I realize now that narcissists gain pleasure when we feel hurt. This type of verbal abuse also infuses the gaslighting tactic because if you question or react to an appalling remark, the narcissist usually says, "it's just a joke. Geez. Why are you so sensitive?" which then makes you doubt yourself.
Do this:
Regardless of the situation, learn to stand up for yourself. You don't have to be aggressive or physical about it, just clearly communicate what you can and cannot tolerate. Call out the manipulative narcissist on his or her game and let them know it is not okay. Distance yourself from such people and avoid any further interactions if possible.

9. Control.

Malignant narcissists want to control everything. The conversation, the meals, the social outings, finances - literally everything. But the most important thing they love gaining control over is your emotional state. They love toying with your emotions. Disagreements about trivial things, rage, and conflicts that come from nowhere are all tactics to keep your emotions off balance. They will emotionally withdraw and the re-idealize you once they feel like they're losing you and keep swinging from the false self to the true self to keep you on the emotional edge. Psychologically you can never feel sure about who your partner really is.
The more power a narcissist has over your emotions, the less likely you'll trust in your own reality, whether it's a parental or intimate relationship.

Do this:

Seek out help so you can reclaim your emotional power and take back control in your life. Find your power once more because it's the only way people will cease to control and take advantage of you.

Chapter 05: The science and psychology behind narcissistic relationships

The effects of narcissistic abuse run far deeper than physical harm. In fact, modern science has proven that consistent emotional trauma over a long period can cause victims to develop both PTSD and C-PTSD. There are also detrimental physical effects on the brain when one is suffering from consistent emotional abuse. Medical scientists have found that victims experience a shrinking of the hippocampus and a swelling of the amygdala, both of which carry serious consequences.

Your brain on trauma

The hippocampus: This is the part of your brain responsible for short-term memory. Information is stored in short-term memory before it gets converted to permanent memory. Without short-term memory, learning becomes very difficult.
In a study from Stanford University and the University of New Orleans, they found there was a strict correlation between high levels of cortisol (a stress-induced hormone) and decreased volume in the hippocampus. The more stressed a person is, the smaller their hippocampus becomes.

The Amygdala: This is the part of our brain responsible for our fight or flight reaction. Also known as the reptilian brain, it controls our primal emotions and functions including fear, hate, lust as well as our breathing and heart rate.

Malignant narcissists usually create an atmosphere for their victims where the amygdala is continually stimulated and continuously on the alert. This is very detrimental to the well-being of the victim and often results in a permanent state of anxiety and fear. Even after the victim survives such a horrid experience they will continue to have PTSD symptoms, increased phobias, panic attacks and so on because their enlarged amygdala is so used to seeking out and experiencing that state of fear.

Unfortunately, the psychological harm and effects of being exposed to narcissistic abuse, whether physical or emotional or both can push your brain activity beyond the zone of effectiveness. A damaged hippocampus can cripple everything you do, learn, and impede your progress. This is because the brain needs to create new neural pathways to learn new things, and that process usually takes place in the hippocampus. But if you're releasing too much cortisol all the time due to the stressful nature of your relationship, the cortisol will attach the neurons in the hippocampus (causing it to shrink) and stimulate the amygdala which in turn affects your thoughts and mental activity so that instead of being focused, productive and happy, you feel stressed, constantly worried and fearful of everything.

Why the emotional and psychological abuse?

Narcissists crave and depend on validation and praise from the external world. When you are a loving, giving sensitive person it's only natural that you'll generously give what the narcissist wants and although at a surface level this doesn't seem like such a bad story, the underlying consequences of a prolonged relationship that's one-sided and solely focused on satiating the monster needs of another are anything but positive. It's almost impossible to create a healthy balanced, nourishing relationship when in a relationship with a narcissist whether they genuinely care about you or not.

We like to believe that loving another means accepting them fully just as they are with flaws and all. That it's not our place to try and make people become what they are not but simply love them as they are. But what this does is create an incredibly negative experience for us where we feel stuck in something detrimental to our well-being and happiness. The psychological abuse becomes inevitable when dealing with a narcissist because you won't always be able to live up to their endless demands and needs. As soon as you don't fit into their plans, their nature is to punish and inflict pain in whatever way possible. Because everything is about them, they will never listen to your needs and will tend to downplay your interests and feelings, which alone becomes the start of an unhealthy relationship. I believe that the main reason behind the pain and suffering narcissists inflict has something to do with their inability to connect and love another human being deeply. A narcissist's heart either hasn't developed or has been shut down due to early psychic trauma such as being raised by narcissistic parents.

It is this crippling handicap both emotionally and spiritually that hinders their ability to connect and dims their intuitive guidance, empathic abilities, and love.

Narcissistic supply

This is a concept that was introduced into psychoanalytic theory by Otto Fenichel in 1938. It's typically used in a negative sense to describe the excessive need a malignant narcissist has for attention, praise, and admiration from others. Simply stated, narcissistic supply is energy, and it's what you are feeding your abuser as long as you're active in the relationship. It can be positive energy in the form of compliments, praise and affection or negative energy in the form of arguments, fights, etc.

You give them attention, validate their ideas, and in a weird way, keep their false self alive and powerful. I know they like to call you needy, but the truth is, they need you for their own survival. Narcissists need to suck energy and attention from people to feel alive, and they need a constant distraction to drown out their inner screams of defectiveness and dysfunction. The more they get supplied, the more they want it and will continue to play their mind games until they feel they've had enough then it'll be time to move on to the next supplier.

I see it more like a drug for the narcissist because this "supply" is what provides the emotional life force they need without which they would probably self-destruct. I believe it is the reason behind all their manipulative and abusive actions. When a narcissist spots a potential supplier, which is usually someone vulnerable to narcissistic abuse or other types of trauma, they see that as an open opportunity to get ahead, and you can be sure, they will stop at nothing to get their daily supply.

Now that you understand the narcissist in your life has a false self to recognize that this false self is dependent on gaining validation, praise, and admiration to confirm its existence. This is usually achieved through external means because the narcissist is unable to generate a sense of wholeness from within. As a consequence of paying the ultimate price for the disowned inner self, he or she seeks out external supply in the form of narcissistic victims.

In deeply contemplating why malignant narcissists love to abuse their victims I have come to the conclusion that it is because they need to feel alive and the only way they know how to do it is by putting others down and taking from them the healthy emotional energy they sense from their victim in an attempt to fill the void within. In other words, "supply me with the version of me that is missing, so I can escape the "dead" inner version of myself." Makes sense, doesn't it?

The cycle of abuse

Highly experienced narcissists seduce their prey without ever touching them. They learn your love language quickly and know how to appeal to what you enjoy hearing. Winning your love is a great distraction (to their hidden issues) that they truly enjoy. As they draw you into their trap there's no end to the foreplay both verbal and physical they are willing to do, and in this chivalry, most of us fall head over heels for these charming devils. There seems to be a clear cycle that most narcissists take their victims through. Sometimes I wonder if there's a manual written for them that the rest of us are unaware of. Here's the cycle of doom that usually leaves the narcissist's prey in utter despair.

Idealization and love-bombing:

This phase can best be described as ecstasy for both the narcissist and the victim, especially in intimate relationships. During this phase, the narcissist will give constant attention and affection, excessive praise, flattery, and put us up on a pedestal. For many of us, we blindly fall for this tactic and unknowingly become devoted and times disturbingly close to worshiping them. The words and actions of the narcissist though hollow seem too good to pass up and we begin to invest everything. Malignant narcissists do a great job mirroring our needs and deepest desires; sometimes even our interests and points of view.

Soon enough, the hope of a brighter loving future and your dream relationship starts to feel like the only possible reality, and you get addicted to the showers of affection. If it's an intimate relationship, the romance and lovemaking are heavenly, and you can't get enough of it. It's filled with just the right amount of tenderness and aggression, and the narcissist really knows how to bring you to greater heights. Bonding takes place, and you assume the feeling is genuine and mutual. It feels like you just met your soul mate; your twin flame; the one you were made for.

The connection is so heightened during this love-bombing phase it causes you to invest your spiritual, emotional, physical and even biological attention and before too long you're relying on this new fantastic person for survival, and that's when trouble begins.

During this idealization phase, the cracks within the mask that the narcissist is wearing start to show, but most people are too smitten to notice the signs. Those who are lucky and super mindful might pick up on it and recognize the empty shell beneath all the charm and quickly exit the fatal relationship, but this is still rare. For more of us, even if the false masks slip occasionally and we get a sneak peek of the true self of the narcissist, we don't realize what's happening until things are deep and dark.

Devaluation:

This phase usually begins with a shift that you can "feel" but not easily articulate. You're not sure why or how but something changes. He or she cuts down communication and becomes withdrawn and moody. With other people, they seem to be acting the same, but with you, something is definitely off. The playful, flirtatious nature and praises that used to be yours now pass over and land on the ears of others. Instead of the endless affection and attention, you start getting criticism, harsh insults, and sudden inexplicable outbursts. When he or she pulls away, it's with great force and lack of concern, and you start to see how much they enjoy humiliating you. They enjoy provoking you, making you jealous and bringing in others into the dynamic of your relationship, whether that's an ex, a friend, etc.

Then there's the stone-cold silence after stonewalling you during arguments. You literally feel that invisible solid wall placed between you two as they go into full mode silent treatment. I find it to be an inexplicable sense of being trapped yet tethered as you ache for the person you first met.

Being devalued makes you feel like you're worthless. The verbal and emotional battery inflicted by a narcissistic abuser shreds your self-esteem and saturates your mind with disempowering belief systems and messages of unworthiness.

Living feels like a battle that never ends.

The Discard:

Even if you find a way to escape a relationship with a malignant narcissist the problem doesn't end there because most of them tend to stalk and harass their victims even years later especially if you're dealing with a vindictive type.
For the victims that don't find a way to escape before it's too late, a horrific trauma is what awaits them once the narcissist chooses to dispose of them. After having your mind, body, and soul violated used and destroyed by someone you believed to be a perfect soul mate, you are then subjected to the ultimate betrayal that hinders you from having closure in the relationship.

This discard phase is often very painful humiliating and unforgettable for the victim. In such cases, one is left feeling depleted, drained, belittled, diminished, and with more questions than answers; more doubt than certainty. It's no wonder so many victims of narcissistic abuse fall into depression and suffer symptoms of trauma. In some cases, victims have even committed suicide because they just couldn't deal with reality after such an ordeal.

Unfortunately, most people are not familiar with the cycle of abuse, and they have very little understanding of what the abuser's world is like. This means that for the most part, after facing such a traumatic experience, the victim will tend to blame himself or herself for being abused. But as you read this, I want to assure you, this is far from the whole truth. A narcissistic abuser or any type of abuser would continue to hurt and harm people whether you were around or not. Their unresolved wounds and issues are not your fault.

In 1979 Leonor Walker made an illustration that is very useful in helping us understand how we got stuck in an abusive relationship and why it's so hard to get out.

Tension building: This is where the abuser turns into a grumpy frowning person always finding any reason to poison the air around you. They become pissed at everything, nothing you do seems right, and they have this glare in their eyes.

The incident: This is where the malignant narcissist has an outburst. Narcissistic rage is the common term, and for most of them, name-calling and other verbal abuse are used. Some even go to the extreme of physical abuse at this point. For example, I once worked with a client who was healing from an extremely narcissistic father. It had taken him years to forgive and mend the broken relationships in their family, and one time, he shared with me some stories of when his dad would have "rage episodes." He would go from sheep to wolf in an instant, and although he never physically laid hands on him or his mom, the guy would punch the wall or smash the windscreen of his car in a total rage.

The reconciliation: For the malignant narcissist, reconciliation just means being able to justify their outburst and rage. It is usually a combination of blaming it on something or someone else and playing the victim.

The calm phase: This phase happens when the narcissist gets distracted and temporarily gets consumed by a new interest. This can be a new relationship, a promotion at work, traveling, or some other self-serving experience. If you happen to be the reason for their distraction, then you'll be encountering the narcissist at their very best, which means you may not quickly detect that you are dealing with a narcissist. But what exactly are you distracting them from?
Their own anger. Malignant narcissists and all types of abusers are outraged people, and they lash out at other people because they don't know how to handle with their inner turmoil.

When you first interact with a malignant narcissist whether it's an adult to an adult relationship or if you were born to a narcissistic parent, things were great because you were their distraction. It helped him, or her feel good to be distracted by you but over time as life happens cracks start showing up, and you (the distraction) stopped being enough for them to suppress all the anger that was bubbling underneath. All of a sudden, he or she becomes a different person. You start to experience some tension building even though you don't know why, they become irritable, edgy, and the same things they used to praise about you become unbearable to them.

And of course, the cycle begins for them in your presence. It never crosses your mind that the person may just be an angry narcissist; instead, you try your best to come to their rescue to get things back into that calm phase.

Having read this far, I can assure you, the best and only path left after such an ordeal is the long road to healing and reclaiming personal power. If you are tired of being entangled in the games of a narcissist and you want to make sure it never happens to you or someone you care about, healing yourself is the only way forward. You must make sure to take necessary measures so that you don't get sucked back into that pit of drama, despair, and abuse.

Chapter 06: Narcissism at work and in relationships

Narcissistic relationships, whether with parents, loves, or colleagues, can make life utterly miserable. People suffering from any type of disorder but especially malignant narcissism carry tremendous pain deep within but they pretend it's not there and instead prefer to lash out and punish other people just to ease their pain. They are not willing to deal with the pain and anger in their lives, so they are constantly battling it out in very unhealthy ways that harm people around them. One of the main coping mechanisms they use is to mute out their empathy or compassion for other people. They learned not to show emotions or get vulnerable with anyone, which hinders their ability to connect and care for another human being genuinely. If you have been raised by a narcissist or currently feel stuck in a narcissistic relationship either at work or in your private life, I want to help you find a way out and be free mentally, emotionally, physically and spiritually.

Narcissistic parents

Being the child of a narcissist is tough. You exist to make your parent look good and to serve their endless demands. Children of narcissists endure years of psychological anguish before reaching the painstaking realization that something is very wrong. Of course, not all children grow up to make this connection, and so chances of healing from it are minimal. Clinical psychologist Dr. Seth Meyers said, "The reality of narcissistic parenting couldn't be sadder. The child of the narcissist realizes early on that he exists to provide a reflection for the parent and to serve the parent- not the other way around. The problem with being a child of a narcissist is that it takes these children so many years of frustration and anguish to figure out that mom or dad isn't quite right. Until that point, these children are merely dancing as fast as they can, trying to please the impossible-to-please narcissist parent. It takes years to finally see that the type of parenting they've been receiving is wrong if not emotionally abusive."
That was my story as a child of a narcissistic dad. And when I finally did a little digging and realized my mom was coming from a long line of victims of narcissistic abuse, I couldn't take it anymore. I decided it needed to end with me before I passed on the same belief systems and

tendencies to my future children. There's no doubt about it, growing up as a victim of narcissistic abuse alters the way you grow up and perceive yourself in the world.

A member of my online community who also grew up with a narcissistic parent said that she spent her entire childhood wishing mom would go away and that whenever they were at home, she was always praying someone would come to visit so the insults and mockery would subside for a while. Her mom was incapable of genuinely showing interest or acknowledging anything good in her daughter. Even her most significant accomplishments at school were downplayed. Like many of us, she felt utterly unworthy and undeserving of affection or genuine praise. People treating her with kindness totally freaked her out because her mom had only exposed her to mockery and mistreatment.

How do narcissistic parents see their children?

As long as you are not perceived as a threat by your narcissistic mom or dad and as long as you can make them proud, they'll be okay towards you. They see you as an extension of themselves. Usually, when you're young, there are lesser issues because you haven't yet become an independent thinker. Trouble grows as you get older because the moment you become difficult or can't live up to their expectations then you become an obstacle, a problem they must deal with.

I could go on and on about the trauma of growing up with narcissistic parents but rather than dig deeper into wounds you know all too well, let's focus our attention on how to deal with our parents during our journey of healing.

It's not likely that you can completely eliminate all contact from your parent because even in the case of death, if that wound is still active you will continue to experience their presence in your mind and worse still you may attract more relationships that are similar to that old one. Therefore, it's not a question of running away, but rather, how can you permanently heal and gain freedom? And once you have found your freedom, how do you deal with them when necessary? Here's my solution for this:

- Start by self-reflection to see how your parental relationship influences your behavior.

Before you can start the journey of freedom and rewrite your destiny, you need to do the uncomfortable work of looking within to see how badly the narcissist has affected you in your life. Then you must diffuse those aspects so that he or she can have less power over you. Things like fear of disappointing your parent, difficulty expressing your feelings and desires, fearing his or her tantrums and rage episodes are all signs that you were raised by a narcissistic parent. You've probably adapted yourself over the years to cope with these signs, and your parent now understands how to press your buttons. Dr. Alan Rappaport says that co-narcissistic people, as a result of their attempt to get along with their narcissistic parents work hard to please others, defer to other's opinions, worry about how others think and feel about them, are often depressed or anxious, find it hard to know their own views and experience and take the blame for interpersonal problems.

So once you are brave enough to recognize the damage that has been inflicted choose to educate, empower, and heal yourself. I always recommend seeking professional help first because that's what worked for me. The fact that we are dealing with childhood trauma makes it difficult to overcome the entire experience on your own and catching your own blind spots is impossible so best to find a professional that you can trust who is trained to deal with such sensitive matters.

- Recognize that you are dealing with abnormal parental behavior.

Don't just gloss over your situation as stressful. I know as children, we all want to do right by our parents, and usually, we desire to find a mutually beneficial way of fixing our dysfunctional family. But when dealing with a person suffering from a narcissistic personality disorder, the option of mutually beneficial doesn't exist. It's always going to be their way or the high way.

In my family drama, my father demanded that I either do things his way or hit the road and goodness me that was the best decision I ever made in my life. It was the beginning stages of me escaping the trap of his abuse.

- **Refuse to be gaslighted anymore.**

It is a common thing for malignant narcissists to try to convince their children that they are crazy and delusional. If your parent is continually telling you that you're being loony or that your version of events is the wrong one, then it's time you stopped doubting yourself and trust more in your thoughts. This doesn't mean that you'll always recall everything with perfect accuracy but what I want to drive home for you is that your ability to interpret and define what's real to you should be in your power to control. Don't let your reality be dictated by someone who is always looking to be right and have things their way.

- **Accept that friends and other family relatives may not understand your situation.**

Unless someone has experienced being with a narcissist, it's tough to get him or her to see the hidden abuse you might be undergoing. More often than not, the narcissist is so charming and normal (wearing their mask) in front of other people that it's hard to receive full support or help from them. They'll often say "she'll come around" or "she's the only mother you'll ever have." That's why I encourage you to seek professional help or a community of other survivors and healing victims. Don't feel guilty for taking action to heal and protect yourself even if others don't agree with the extensive measures you take.

- **Set firm boundaries.**

A malignant narcissist usually has no respect for personal boundaries, so you'll find your parent overstepping reasonable boundaries just to prove they are in control. You are allowed to have your own life and your individual needs and desires. Since a narcissistic parent cannot understand this, establish boundaries that protect your well-being, and make sure you include the necessary consequences of violating said boundaries.

• Silence that inner critic.

The learned voice of internal judgment is perhaps the biggest poison that will eat at you if you don't do something about it. And have you noticed that voice sounds just like your parent? In fact, it was likely nurtured by him or her. This is why running away from narcissistic abuse doesn't necessarily give you freedom and peace of mind. That constant reminder that you are not good enough or that you will never be loveable can be profoundly damaging to a child. Children who are raised with this frame of mind usually struggle to see their self-worth or believe in their own potential. Over time this turns into a powerful belief that continues to recreate itself as reality. It can take years of work to take the sting out of such a belief, and the crazy part is that even if you know it's not true, it can still haunt you.

• Understand that you may need to cut ties with your parent and move on.

Many victims of narcissistic abuse feel a sense of responsibility like they have to make things work. I have found this usually doesn't end well. Even if you estrange yourself from your parent, if the guilt of doing it taunts you and you end up going back to fix the broken relationship out of guilt, nothing good will come out of that. Your parent will still continue to manipulate, control, and cause harm to your life.

A friend experienced this when she went back to try to fix her relationship after a six-year estrangement. Six months into the newly formed relationship, it became apparent to her that nothing had changed. Nothing was going to improve because her mother did not see this as a second chance or new beginning. Instead, it was an opportunity to get revenge on the six years they were apart. Because it had been many years of being free from the influence of the narcissistic mother, she quickly caught sight of the manipulation that was taking place and lovingly stepped back, this time for good.

"After six months of earnest effort trying to mend our relationship, I realized we had reached the end of the road. I was hoping to have a healthy mother-daughter relationship, but all she wanted was someone to manipulate, and I'm no longer interested in filling that role. So I said goodbye, this time for good and even though I haven't fully made peace with my mother, I do feel I have closure, and I certainly feel more at peace with the absence of my mother."

Narcissistic partners and how to free yourself How to break up with a narcissist

It's now clear that you're in a relationship with someone who is no good for you and you want out. The relationship is exhausting, confusing and saps life force out of you yet you're still in it why?

Malignant narcissists are professional manipulators and so charming it's hard for us to realize what's going on without a little education. Hopefully, at this point, you've learned enough about narcissists to figure out where you're in a relationship with one. And if you are, it's time to liberate yourself.

1. Don't fall for the manipulation tactics any longer.
Now that you know the manipulation tricks and tools they use try to be more aware when the narcissist attempts to use them to draw you into the narcissistic vortex again. Remember narcissists are really convincing, persuasive, and persistent when they want something. If you feel ready to leave, be decisive, stick to your convictions, and move on to a more positive future where you can expect to receive real love.

2. Focus on the future.
Once you've detached from the narcissist, don't look back. It is imperative to focus all your energy on positive empowering forward momentum and activities that make you feel alive. Work on finding yourself and reclaiming your power not justifying the actions of the narcissist.

3. Detach yourself from the need to fix the narcissist or get all your questions answered.
Again, this is something you need to be super wary of because most victims get stuck in a loop long after the relationship has ended. It may not always be easy, but you must silence that voice that wants to keep digging for answers. Let go of the dead past and keep your word to yourself that you will cut all ties permanently.

4. Be kind to yourself.

As you heal and restore your identity and sense of worth, it is essential you show yourself compassion. Learn to forgive yourself. Be kind to yourself and reinforce the belief that you are worthy of a better, more loving relationship. Self-love and self-compassion is the start of all healing, and your future relationships can only get better if you work on loving yourself.

Narcissism at work

There are specific behavior patterns that you'll learn to recognize when dealing with narcissists at work. These people love to create chaos, they are always looking for praise and validation and want other people to do their tasks for them. They like forming clicks, getting ahead, and are usually unhealthily competitive. They do all these things intentionally, and if you let them get to you, they'll quickly claw their way into your mind and start sucking energy from you.

If you've realized you're dealing with a co-worker, subordinate or a boss who is a narcissist, here are some tips to help you cope and handle them better without harming your own sense of wellbeing.

• Manage your own ego and expectations.

With the clear understanding, you have acquired of how narcissism works and how fragile a narcissist's ego is, it's crucial you set the right expectations for yourself. Manage your need to win or be right and learn to heal yourself so that you don't expect too much from such a person. Don't expect a narcissist to see or agree with your point of view or to be thoughtful. Recognize the situation you are in and act mindfully and accordingly to ensure you come off it with the least amount of blows.

• Don't name-call or label them as a narcissist.

Unless you are a medical professional, it's ethically wrong to label anyone anything. Besides, they won't take it very well and might have the perfect reason to exercise revenge if you threaten their self-image.

- Keep your calm when dealing with the narcissist.

Don't react to their drama and don't engage with them beyond what you have to do to get the task accomplished.

- Be clear about what the role is for each of you and what the expectations are. Whether it's you assigning the task or receiving the assignment, make sure you both have clarity on who is doing what so that everyone knows their responsibilities.

- Don't give them personal information.

They don't care about you or your feelings, so don't express your vulnerability as this will only harm you in the end. Stay focused on the project at hand, keep conversations short,, and purely focused on completing whatever is on the agenda.

- Keep records and openly track the progress of your working partnership.

To help keep things open and avoid the conflict of responsibility, I recommend you record and track everything involved in your working partnership. If it's a project, you're working on together keep open track of it. If it's a meeting, write it down or record it or do it over emails so that all members concerned have records of what's happening and what needs to happen.

These are just a few tips you can customize to suit your particular situation so that you can learn to co-exist with the narcissist at work. I firmly believe that a narcissist should not adversely impact your career, project, or company. With this knowledge, you now have the power to make sure that person never stands in the way of your success.

Whether you are dealing with a narcissistic parent, spouse, colleague, friend, or lover, know that you are not alone in your experience. There are many helpful articles, books, and people sharing their stories online. Find a support group if you don't feel like taking professional therapy. Do your best to start to educate and empower yourself so you can begin healing and enjoying personal freedom and peace of mind.

Chapter 07: How Past Wounds Make Us Susceptible To Toxic Narcissists

Most victims of narcissistic abuse want to know whether their childhood upbringing had anything to do with the fact that they continue to fall into abusive intimate relationships. Sadly, the short answer is yes.

Those of us who experienced traumatizing childhood experiences have wounds, which could be unconsciously leading us to attract the very things we want to escape. For example, if you grew up in a home where you experienced physical abuse from your dad, you'll likely grow up to be a person that attracts lovers who abuse you too. And if you're not the one being abused, you might develop tendencies of lashing out and physically abusing your partners.

But there is something I want to be very clear about. I am not here to point fingers or play the blame game. Just because you grew up a victim of early childhood trauma doesn't mean you should now spend the rest of your life blaming your parents for your messed up life. Our parents may not have given us an environment that supported healthy childhood experiences, but blaming them will not get us any closer to healing. Both your parents did the best job they knew how with the level of consciousness they had. They were most likely victims of traumatic experiences too, given how prevalent unconscious parenting has been in previous generations.

So is it enough to have read this book or articles on the web to help you escape the horrors of narcissistic abuse permanently? Well, reading this book is a starting point, and it does set you on the path of healing, but real and holistic healing can only come from rectifying the traumatic emotional imprints of our childhood. Only when this happens can we develop a stable and healthy inner identity, which is no longer susceptible to abuse.
Before you can be able to make the connection with how your past has led you to your present and made you a target for narcissistic abuse, let's lay some essential foundations.

What is trauma?

Trauma is the inability to deal with a specific stressful situation, which in turn causes feelings of overwhelm and powerlessness. It happens when one isn't able to process stressful events, experiences, and circumstances to completion and implement a proper resolution. This unresolved tension turns into stress, gets internalized, and becomes stored as a traumatic memory that eventually begins to develop a life of its own. As you saw in an earlier chapter, this internalized stress negatively affects our brain and nervous system over time. The more repeated this cycle, the greater the damage. Not only does it affect your mind and body, but it also shapes your belief systems and inner identity. These traumatic beliefs become your reality, and you can easily remain a victim to them your entire lifetime. Why? Because they become a self-fulfilling prophecy that keeps you stuck in a loop replaying the same unhealthy traumatic patterns and disappointments over and over again.

Each time a trigger occurs, your brain immediately activates that stored traumatic experience, which affects your thinking, emotions, and body.

Perhaps you've experienced a trigger moment as heaviness in your chest, feeling nauseated, a shock of cold ice through your vein or you may start shaking and sweating abnormally. All kinds of processes start firing up, and there's a natural impulse to want to flee, fight, defend yourself, or even shut down and literally struggle to think, answer, or move.
In short, unresolved stress in your life will become a trauma.

One of the critical mistakes that you can make regarding the regulation, management, and healing of your past trauma is to think that the solution to your problem needs to be something logical.

When you were little and growing up, the things that your emotional center needed in order to develop healthily include but are not limited to caring physical touch, soothing words of kindness and affection and simply being with you both physically and emotionally. If you didn't actually feel loved, important, valued, and seen for you who are then an impairment was bound to happen that would create an unhealing wound. But the plot thickens even more.

According to modern scientific research on epigenetics tells us that the ability to switch on or off specific genes is something that's inherited. And if we've come from ancestors who've suffered trauma, then the parts of our brain that could handle stress effectively might be shut down from birth. Instead, what we might have are over formed hyper arousal centers and amygdalae which means rather than anchoring into our core identity and personal power to deal with stressful situations, we would disconnect from our powerful inner being and seek solutions externally. The more we seek external solutions and validations, the more powerless we'd feel because our quest to control the uncontrollable would fall flat. Eventually, we'd give up, withdraw, and learn to accept the fractures created which would set us on the cycle of continued trauma and bad experiences.

If you didn't grow up with a functioning and developing core identity (which was dependent on our right brain and nervous system health and formation) and if we didn't have a parent consciously stepping in to do that for us until we fully developed this ability to handle stress, then we started carrying trauma after trauma because we weren't able to integrate stresses to completion.

As children, we were impacted by the disappointments, the fights, things that frightened us, feeling unsafe and uncomfortable but the thing that created the most damage for us was the fact that a safe, functional caretaker didn't show up to help us heal and integrate these stressful situations back to calmness and safety. The overwhelm of not being able to deal with our own emotions caused us to disengage and seek other ways to self-medicate our feelings as we grew so that we didn't have to deal with all the unresolved wounds.
Instead of growing up to be a healthy adult who is connected to his or her own body, emotions, and real inner power, many of us are stuck in a never-ending loop of dysfunction.
I grew up believing that no one was there for me; no one supported or even valued me. As a result, I continued to create this self-fulfilling prophecy attracting people who help validate that reality. Then I would say, "see? I'm right. I have no one in this world who truly loves me for who I am."

Can you relate?

Well, I can assure you, this disempowered reality all happens when we are not yet healed from past wounds. Until we learn to be anchored into our inner core truth and values in our body, it won't be easy to experience being safe and authentically yourself. When we resolve our core trauma through our nervous system the cells in our body, our right brain and our entire being will experience the permanent shift in reality because the old self-defeating belief systems will be deemed obsolete.

Post-traumatic stress disorder is usually the consequence of not healing and continually piling up more traumas while stuck in that imprisoned state. The constant reoccurring unsafe feeling that is all too familiar to victims of trauma isn't just something made up. It's because you're not yet at home within yourself. I used to suffer greatly for many years, and I promise you, it can be healed. I no longer have any of it, and it's only because I went within myself and worked on healing that invisible aspect of me.

You need to reclaim your real power and reconnect yourself body, mind, and soul. It's the only way to get back your compass of life so you can find your true north and discern things, people, and relationships that are healthy and those that aren't.

People who are manipulative and pathological such as malignant narcissists will jump at the chance to toss us around mercilessly. They will pretend to be what we need then use the fact that we are disconnected from ourselves to their advantage so they can profit from our energy, life force, and resources.

As you are starting to awaken now, I urge you to stop trying to monitor and control people, your thoughts, situations, or any other uncontrollable thing outside of you. I also want you to put an end to the false beliefs that were activated during your childhood because all they do is bring pain and more suffering as you go through life.

The only permanent and best way to end the victim lifestyle and abuse that you've had to endure is to awaken and turn inward to do the necessary work essential to your healing. You need to repair and restore yourself where it matters, and that is at your core being.

At this point in the book, healing and taking action on your road to wellness is all that matters. Before I share the six stages of your recovery, I want to end this chapter with a few red flags that malignant narcissists often use to get into your mind. They use these to trigger your unresolved unconscious reactions so you can forever remain a victim at their mercy. Until now, of course.

Five ways Abusive narcissists get to you

Malignant narcissists are like parasitic worms in that they don't want to completely destroy you because they actually need you (and others like you) to survive and get their daily supply, but at the same time, they bring much harm to their host. If you go a long time unknowingly allowing such a parasite to inhabit your body, the consequences might be grievous. Still, many of us have a hard time permanently moving on and healing even when we realize we're not in a healthy relationship.

A friend told me of a time when she used to date this local celebrity DJ who is well known in our city. A few months after they started dating, he slapped her hard on the face for supposedly asking too many questions in a demeaning tone. To be fair, they were both pretty drunk, and it was one of those Friday nights where lots had happened, so she thought nothing of it. Next day, despite the red flag and a swollen right cheek, she decided to let go of the matter, assuming she had overreacted after too many Gin and Tonics. Several weeks went by, and all seemed heavenly again. The guy was so apologetic and wanted to do everything possible to make it up to her, which he did for a while. Then the violent acts of aggression happened again, and again, and again. But each time an episode occurred, the details were so blurry for my friend, she was always left wondering if the entire thing wasn't her fault. Like a parasitic worm, he was harming her and yet she struggled to put an end to things or even acknowledge that something was wrong with him. It was as though she got slowly numbed out over time and became unable to recognize the web of abuse she was living in. The guy was draining life force and self-esteem out of her. He planted the seed of self-doubt and half the time she struggled to believe in her own thoughts. This went on for a long time with bouts of aggressive fighting increasing until one night the outburst was so massive, she ended up in an emergency room at 4 am with a bleeding nose and a black eye. Her parents quickly intervened, forced her to spend some months in recovery with her grandma in a different state, and so began her healing process.

One can only imagine what horrors would have taken place had she continued dating that man. As charming and romantic as he was, her life was in a lot of danger. The biggest obstacle standing in her way of ending things was the fact that she always felt like it was her fault.

This is something many of us experience, and I am convinced it's because malignant narcissists do such a great job getting into our heads. They know how to corrupt and brainwash us into thinking we are the ones doing something wrong.

If you still have an active parasite in your head then whether you've physically left that abusive relationship or not, your healing cannot actually take place. Backsliding and getting sucked into the web of abuse will be all too easy. That's because your abuser still knows how to press all the right buttons to make you succumb. Here are a few tricks you want to become aware of as you start your journey to wellness.

- Malignant narcissists are great at making you think - you are the problem.

As mentioned during the section on manipulation tactics, gaslighting is something many abusers use to control their victims. Your abuser might be convincing you that your perception of the abuse is "all in your head."

You may also get remarks like "you like to provoke me" or "you're too sensitive." This is especially true after a rage episode. He or she will try to plant a seed of doubt and remark upon your emotional instability "your issues" to displace blame of his or her abuse as your fault.

- You're my everything; I can't live without you.

This is something many of us have heard, and it usually works because rather than terminating that relationship for good we find a way to create a repeat cycle of the same abuse that ends in our anguish. How many of us have fallen for this lie over and over? We keep hoping it's going to get better but rarely does it ever get better.

- Malignant narcissists like to say; " I knew I would regret having you in my life."

What this does is it psychologically mess with your innate desire to feel good enough. As crazy as this may sound when your abuser says this to you, it makes you want to cling on to the relationship even more. You'll feel like you must actively stay in that relationship and prove him or her wrong. For example, if you're in an intimate relationship with a narcissist and they say this to you, then you won't want to leave that person because you want to show them how wrong they are and how good you can be. This might cause you to compromise yourself, suppress your ideas, opinions and even let them do ridiculous things such as spend all your money just because you want to show them that you are better than what they claim.

• They will use smear campaigns to press your buttons.

This is where your abuser does everything possible to make it seem as though you're the one who is unstable and causing harm. Smear campaigns get in your head and accomplish three main things. First, you become the abuser or unstable person in your relationship. Second, it triggers and provokes you thus proving your instability to others and lastly, it serves as a hovering technique in which the malignant narcissist tries to suck you back into the traumatic relationship.

• Let's just be friends.

This just means the narcissist wants to keep you in their circle of supply so that whenever they need you, they can just pick you up, use you and discard you as and when necessary. Please don't fall for this one because it's one that really gets to many of us even after we are made aware. Your caring nature and the need to forgive and love everyone should not include actively maintaining a friendship with a malignant narcissist.

" Healing does not mean the damage never existed. It means the damage no longer controls our lives."

Chapter 08: Healing Trauma and permanently detaching

Have you just left or are you currently thinking of leaving an abusive relationship behind but you're just not sure of how to completely let go? Do you find yourself thinking about that person, worrying about them and even feeling like you're missing them even when you don't want to?
Are you asking yourself questions like "Why is taking so long to feel free and healed from this situation?" or "Why do I still love this persona after all they've done to me?" or "Will this pain ever go away?"

A lot of people tell me that even after leaving the relationship they still feel like checking the narcissist's social media updates every hour or they keep feeling like sending a text message to see how they are doing or give them a call to get closure on the relationship. These are all urges that naturally come when you start the journey to freedom, and you must learn to resist them. Obsessing over an emotionally abusive relationship is usually very detrimental to your well-being and causes many to lose their homes, jobs, and even their children. Some people even go as far as attempting suicide and often succeed at it.

I find that most victims and survivors of narcissistic abuse struggle with this aspect of their healing due to one major reason. Namely, they don't learn and practice the art of detachment. It's not always easy, but it's so important you do it when recovering from narcissistic abuse.

What is detachment?

Detachment is a deliberate choice that you make when you're trying to pull yourself away from a toxic relationship. It's a deliberate and conscious decision to no longer be in partnership with the toxic person. But it's important to know that it doesn't just happen all at once. Just because you choose to detach from your narcissistic spouse, for example, doesn't mean it all happens in an instant. It's a starting point, but it will take time, and that's okay especially because frequently there are other complications involved such as children, relatives or business obligations to take care of before one can completely cut out their abuser. In some cases, it's not even possible to cut someone out wholly (which makes detachment even more useful).

Detachment starts to have a positive impact when you consciously refuse to get sucked into the web of lies and manipulative games that a narcissist likes to play. You have to decide that you will no longer accept being demeaned and that you will stand up for yourself when he or she disrespects or belittles you. Because trauma bonding is so addictive, when you do start detaching from your narcissist, it will feel emotionally impossible, and that's why one of the first things you need to do is summon your willpower and cognitive thinking to help you execute. At the start of this, your willpower is what you need to override the emotional patterns, and yes, it will require some effort, but eventually, your emotions will renew and develop their own resilience so that nothing gets to you. But when starting out, focus on the facts and your willpower to avoid getting sucked back into the abuse.

Change begins with you.

If you genuinely want to transform, heal, and rebuild your life after experiencing narcissistic abuse, you have to be willing to change your mind and let go. It all depends on and begins with your intense desire for change and freedom. The more you educate yourself on what a narcissist is and make a conscious effort to strengthen yourself mentally, emotionally, spiritually, and physically, the easier the recovery will be. With awareness comes more possibility and power. You can be able to spot when you're getting sucked into yet another unhealthy relationship or when someone is playing mind games with you. It's also easier to catch yourself repeating old patterns of thought before things get too far. The more empowered you feel, and the more you choose to work on your core healing, the more permanent your new life will be.

If you find yourself always talking about the narcissist and reliving the experiences at every opportunity you get, then you're certainly falling off the path of recovery. If you're still unable to resist the urge to call, text, or stalk them on social media, then for sure, you need help detaching and healing.

Here's what I mean:

Gloria was repeatedly sharing her story over and over again about the state of her traumatizing marriage.

"I realized my husband had NPD years ago and our couples therapist said he had it and referred him to psychotherapy. He has been in therapy, and we are on our 6th psychologist in 8 years. This therapy seemed to help especially EFT but only during the session, and maybe the day after then, he would bounce back. At first, when I started seeing the changes, I finally had hope again. However, he destroys my hope over and over again when he relapses into his old self. He's mean, angry, disrespectful, and rude and has no compassion. In fact, this list could go on and on, but I don't want to dump everything on you guys. I'm done! I've stayed because we have a son. I've left him twice and came back. Now, I know I will walk away and not come back, but I'm afraid of him. His stepson says he is evil. His own 6 years old son says he's a demon. I'm scared of what he will do to my boys or me. I've felt trapped for 8 years. He's in the military, navy seal and due to their "brotherhood," I'm afraid his unit and the public will help only him. But I can't stay. Oh and he says he has PTSD which I totally thought was true, but now I just think he's an a*****e. The good news is I'm onto him. The bad news is he knows I'm weak. Help please!"

Clearly, Gloria is in pain and desperately needs to detach and heal from this trauma before it permanently destroys her. Unfortunately, she is stuck in that same pattern sharing that same story in our community and across social media. Even when she does walk away, it's not long till she finds herself back in the same spot. She is a perfect example of the self-fuelling prophecy that we put lock ourselves in when we don't consciously choose to take responsibility and work on true detachment and healing. Permanently healing from trauma isn't something that can happen by merely venting in a forum or reading a few articles on the topic. It's usually something that requires a great deal of effort, support, professional help, and a strong mindset. Check in with yourself to see where you stand relative to your particular situation. Have you really gotten to the point where you've made a real, deliberate, and conscious decision to make a change?

Have you truly decided to take back your power and heal your identity regardless of how powerful the narcissist has been in your life? Are you willing to change your mind, develop your will power and resist those old urges and triggers that usually keep you stuck? If you answered yes to all the questions, here are six steps I invite you to employ as you start your journey to healing and transformation.

The six steps of your recovery

There are many elements involved during the healing process, and just as with any loss and recovery program, there will be periods of grieving, denial, anger, and even depression. The main difference between a typical breakup and narcissistic abuse recovery, the natural phase of acceptance doesn't naturally follow. Victims of narcissistic abuse usually remain fixated and even obsessed about their abuser, often suffering for decades post-breakup. Some of the stories I have shared with you in this book already alluded to this reality. This partial healing, in turn, keeps them in that repetitive pattern of doom where the only other relationships that can come to fruition during that unhealed phase will be more of the same or similar to the heartache, pain, and abuse they were once subjected to. Needless to say, this is not true healing and certainly doesn't offer the life of freedom and love that I want every survivor to experience after facing narcissistic abuse.

To make sure you completely heal and from your abusive relationship and never again drain your energy obsessing over someone who doesn't deserve your affection, try the following steps.

Step One: Learn grounding techniques and self-soothing methods.

Narcissistic abuse is an emotional trauma that targets your primal abandonment wound as we learned earlier. When you experience betrayal, rejection, and neglect by the narcissist, your amygdala hijacks your rational thinking and triggers your fight, flight, or freeze mode.

For example, the next time you have the thought "I've been rejected because I'm not good enough," a painful emotion will be triggered from that thought that is most likely sadness, depression, panic, etc. The natural instinct that tends to kick in when this happens is to accept and sprint with said emotions like a Running Back on crack with blinders on. I need you to stop in those heated moments and instead create a buffer period that enables you to practice self-soothing methods and grounding techniques that will dampen that emotional hijacking.

While it may not be possible to completely prevent those moments from happening (at least not in the beginning), it is possible to ease your way out of it as soon as you catch yourself getting hijacked. Self-soothing is the most critical step to learn once you start your journey to healing and must be practiced even if you're still in the abusive relationship. The more you can gain power over your emotions and create buffer periods that allow you to breathe, ground yourself, and take charge of your mind, the easier it will be overcome the abusive relationship. Without proper and effective grounding and soothing techniques, any activities you engage in will not yield positive results because your brain will always be hijacked by your wounded amygdala. There are many excellent grounding techniques that you can find online, but here are just a few that many professional therapists advice.

1. Cross your arms, rock, and breathe deeply. Crossing your arms gives you a sense of being contained and supported. Rocking mimics the feeling of being a fetus nestled in the womb, safe from the world. Pair this with slow and deep breathing until you feel powerfully soothed.

2. Gentle hand technique. As soon as you feel yourself getting hijacked by your emotions, close your eyes, and focus on your body. Figure out the part of your body that is experiencing this fear the most. Rest a gentle hand over that part of your body (like a mother would over her little one). This is a form of self-parenting which really helps soothe your inner child. Place your hand there with the intention of pouring unconditional love and light on yourself until you feel the fear dissipating.

3. Say a safety statement to yourself. For example, "My name is [fill in the blank]; I am safe right now. I am in the present, not the past. What I am feeling right now is valid, but I don't need it. I can release and put it away. I am safe right now." If you cannot speak your statement aloud to yourself, then write it down as many times as needed until you feel the shift.

For more grounding and soothing techniques, check out the resources provided at the end of this book.

Step Two: Allow yourself to be angry and grieve.

Just because the relationship with your abuser was one-sided and established on lies doesn't mean you shouldn't allow yourself to grieve, get angry, and experience the pain of it all. The relationship was real for you, regardless of how dysfunctional it was. Not allowing yourself to process these feelings often leads to damaging consequences further down the line. You might end up stuck in an emotional or spiritual rut of bereavement or carry some of that baggage with you to the next relationship. Whenever we don't process and embrace those feelings of anger and grieve, there are usually manifestations that include:
• Feeling emotionless or depressed and sad for prolonged periods of time.
• Prolonged exhaustion, constant fatigue, anxiety, and indifference.
• Falling into one or more addictions as a form of soothing oneself.
• Chronic pain or illness.
• Repeated avoidances.
•Eating disorders and obesity.
• Suppressed anger.

Complicated grief is a serve and long-lasting form of grief that takes over one's life, and unfortunately, it's widespread in the aftermath of an abusive relationship. It is especially true for victims of narcissistic abuse who usually don't get the closure or validation they deserve. That "unfinished business" including unsettled disputes, the discrediting of your character, unanswered questions and unrequited love can leave you hanging and unable to experience completion. Similar to the story I shared earlier of the woman who was left hanging right after getting engaged, that type of experience can leave you feeling stuck in the pain of your grief. This type of grieving is made excruciating by the fact that you have to grieve twice. First for the person who love-bombed you and for whom you fought to bring back amidst soul-shattering abuse and second, you grieve for the end of the relationship.

If you believe you're suffering from any psychological neurosis or complicated grief, then I urge you to seek professional help from a therapist who specializes in abuse and trauma before it's too late. Sometimes you might even have to go on prescribed medication but make sure to inquire about non-addictive types that you can use on those unbearable days. Complicated grief used to be associated strictly with bereavement, but medical professionals now agree that it can apply to any kind of traumatic loss, so please reach out for help if you need it.

Step Three: Stop researching obsessively on narcissism.

I know many bloggers, vloggers, and speakers on this topic will keep saying you need to educate yourself as much as possible and talk about your suffering on as many platforms, chat rooms, and forums as you can, but here's the thing: If you're wanting to transform, heal and restart your life, digging into the old wounds only keeps that reality alive and active.

This isn't to say you should be ignorant. During the awakening and discovery phase, you absolutely need to gain understanding about narcissism, why your partner or parent behaves as they do, what traits make them identifiable, and so on. It's essential in helping you recognize the dynamics of your abusive relationship. But that is just the first phase. Once you awaken and gain awareness, it's time to shift your focus. When it's truly time to heal yourself, you should then place all your attention on the actual healing and the actions you can take. Self-care, self-love, accessing your inner power, reclaiming your identity, processing traumatic emotions, and other healing methods should be the only thing you care about.

Continuing to research on the traits of your narcissistic parent or disordered ex keeps your focus on them, not your healing and recovery. Dr. Dan Siegel, a neuroscientist, often likes to remind us that what fires together, wires together. That's how our brain creates new neural pathways. Each time we repeat a particular thought or action, we are in essence reinforcing the connection between our neurons, which in turn keeps those thoughts active and sees that as the lifestyle we want more of. This is how our day-to-day reality is shaped.

I know this will be difficult to fully implement in the early stages because you'll be rewriting your old thought patterns and beliefs. Shifting from making your abuser the center of your world to making yourself the center of your world is actually easier said than done. But I want you to take it a day at a time and put as much effort as is necessary. Use your willpower to put an end to devoting your attention on the narcissist and train your mind to focus on improving your own life.

Step Four: Develop your self-esteem.

At this point, you want to come to the realization that regardless of the torment, degradation, and rejection, the narcissist put you through; who you are is a powerful being. The perceived identity that was broken by your abuser isn't who you are; you are far more than that. No one can ever really hurt or define your real identity, expect you.

The primary goal of a malignant narcissist is to make you feel invalidated, invisible, and unworthy. So even if the narcissist does actually love being around you and think the world of you, they would never admit it unless they want to take advantage of it in some way. The more you can believe that you're not worthy of love and that you're "damaged goods," the more a narcissist will easily keep you around. They've learned that by destroying your self-esteem and making you feel useless, keeping you around becomes easy.

Step Five: Incorporate movement into your daily routine.

Whether you resonate with Yoga, running, dancing, or other forms of physical activity, releasing endorphins is a crucial step in this healing process. It will help you feel safe and stable and generate the positive feelings that have been torn down from emotional trauma.

I know when in the midst of the pain and suffering, it can be hard to believe that one day you'll experience happiness and love again but trust me, the heart does heal. You just need to foster an environment conducive for healing and physically engaging your body helps create such an atmosphere. Love yourself enough to believe that you deserve refuge from pain, abuse, and suffering.

Step Six: Work on reconnecting with your passion and purpose in life.

Frequently the path to complete healing is impeded by the past and repeated cycles of backsliding. I firmly believe that if you choose to focus on your future and invest your time, energy, and resources going after something that brings you deep meaning and satisfaction, things will fall into place much faster. Even the cravings of your abuser won't have such a significant hold on you because you can quickly refocus on the new idea or project that makes you come alive. Find something that brings you joy and makes you feel like you are making a difference in the world. Something that is bigger than you and even feels impossible to attain at this point in time. Keep your eye on that as you go through the journey of healing and sooner rather than later, you'll discover the old life has fallen off, and your new life is taking shape.

This takes time, practice, determination, and a clear plan. It also requires a lot of self-love, self-care, and the desire to make something good out of your life. Speaking of which, if you're not sure where to start when it comes to practicing self-love and self-care, try some of the tips I am sharing next.

Five self-care suggestions that are integral to your complete healing and transformation

Self-compassion and self-care are integral cornerstones of healing from an abusive relationship. It is often easier said than done because for many of us, learning to love ourselves and see ourselves as special, is one of the most challenging tasks we face.

When you've spent your whole life in a dark place, feeling invisible and worthless, it can be tough replacing that image of yourself with feelings of adoration and love, but that is precisely what you must do to heal and transform your life fully. You must give yourself the gift of love, affection, and adoration because ironically, being able to attract true love and being able to love others well depends on your ability to love yourself. You must retrain your mind to give yourself the very things your narcissistic abuser has tried to take away from you. By practicing self-care and extending love toward yourself, you begin to cultivate feelings of self-worth, strength, and resilience, which is precisely what you need to overcome trauma and narcissistic abuse.

Loving yourself is not selfish or self-centered. I hope you know that. Pointing your compassion inwards fosters increased empathy for those around you and enables you to heal those deeply hidden wounds from your past. When I speak of self-care, I mean every aspect of your being. You need to design for yourself a balanced lifestyle to aid you on this journey of recovery, and that includes exercise, proper nutrition, getting enough sleep, etc. It's also about exerting healthy boundaries for yourself and others, especially the narcissists in your life that you can't completely avoid either due to family or legally binding obligations.

Self-care is also about developing a mindfulness attitude so that you can become more aware of your thoughts, behaviors, and the things that trigger you as well as your behaviors and actions.If you're in resonance with everything I just said, here are some key elements of self-care I encourage you to practice on this journey of recovery and transformation.

1. Physical self-care.

This implies caring for your physical body, both internally and externally. This includes things like
• Getting enough sleep.
• Regularly taking long walks in nature or on the beach.
• Eating healthy, nourishing, wholesome meals.
• Drinking plenty of water.
• Eliminating or reducing beverages that over stimulate your nervous system.
• Exercising and moving your body regularly so you can optimize your energy levels.

2. Emotional self-care.

This is especially important for those of us subjected to trauma and narcissistic abuse. Being able to take back control of our emotions so we can stop being manipulated and emotionally chained to unhealthy situations is paramount to our healing.

You can take care of your emotional well being by processing and verbalizing feelings with trusted friends, a coach, healer, or a professional therapist who specializes in trauma and abuse. You can also release negative emotions through an expressive art form, such as:

- Drawing.
- Painting.
- Listening to music.
- Dancing.
- Singing.
- Playing an instrument.
- Pottery.
- Poetry etc.

One of my closest friends started taking art classes to release the emotional block that had been tormenting her life since childhood. The anger she carried for her narcissistic mother slowly started dissolving when she started even though she wasn't very good at it. Over time, she's not only graduated to an advanced class, but she's also emotionally transformed radiating a happier, lighter and more passionate side that I had never encountered before.

Of course, it also helps that she learned to fully incorporate the technique I will be sharing with you on the next chapter because, at the end of the day, freedom from narcissistic abuse is best enjoyed when one can eliminate situations that cause undue emotional distress. By releasing instead of suppressing your emotions, you can move through painful experiences that may otherwise keep you stuck in permanent suffering.

3. Mental self-care.

Victims and survivors of narcissistic abuse absolutely need this type of self-care. After all, the whole game behind a malignant narcissist is to break you mentally so that you can feel helpless in their power and depend on them. Practice self-care by trying new activities that challenge and stimulate you intellectually. Things like

• Listening to an empowering thought-provoking podcast.
• Completing a puzzle.
• Engaging in deep, inspiring, and meaningful conversation with a friend.
• Immerse yourself in a book that empowers you like Brené Brown's "The Gifts Of Imperfection: Let Go Of Who You Think You're Supposed To Be And Embrace Who You Are."

4. Social self-care.

Although narcissistic abuse makes us more wary of opening up to more relationships, we still need to nurture real relationships with individuals who uplift and support us. Whether it is with a therapist, friend, family member, or community members, create a support system around you and build strong and meaningful relationships. Cut all ties with old relationships that keep you feeling like a victim. A few ways to meet and nurture great social connections could be:

• Volunteering at special events.
• Joining a healing or yoga class.
• Joining a recovery program.
• Joining a mastermind group.

5. Spiritual Self-care.

There is no right or wrong way to practice this form of self-care, and each person will need to develop their own ritual based on held beliefs and religious preferences. For some, spirituality is found in the wilderness; for others, it's found in books or retreats. Your spirituality is going to be personal to you and only you. The core thing is to generate feelings of connectedness, oneness, wholeness, and universality. True healing is about coming into your true identity and healing yourself at the very core of your being, and that will require spiritual integration. So figure out what brings you into that space and diminishes loneliness, self-doubt, fear and all other lower states of being. A few practices have been known to bring victims of narcissistic abuse into a place of wholeness. Here are a few suggestions to test out.

- Meditation.

I consider meditation to be one of the easiest and best ways to connect to the spiritual aspect of yourself. Of course, it requires a little effort and commitment, in the beginning, to keep going especially because one generally feels like nothing is happening. When I first started meditating, my thoughts were drowning me, I kept wondering if I was doing it right, and I was doing it with the aim of "making something happen." Here's the thing with meditation - it's not about making something happen; it's about just being with yourself in the present moment and simply basking in your own awareness. So I encourage you to start slowly, for a few minutes each day and soon enough you'll notice many changes taking place within and eventually on the outside as well. I assure you, the benefits of meditation are life changing, including, rewiring your brain's neural activity, reducing stress and giving you more clarity. Once you get the hang of it, you won't be able to imagine life without some daily mediation.

- Yoga.

The intention behind yoga is to harmonize your body, mind, and spirit, and it's usually individualized according to what your needs are at the time. Most people recognize yoga as a form of workout, which is good because indeed it has physical health benefits, but there's more to it than this. For recovering victims and survivors, yoga is especially wonderful at helping us connect with our body and emotions stored deep within.

I encourage you to give it a try for a couple of weeks. It will help you practice non-judgment and self-acceptance with your current situation, which is one of the most challenging things to do when starting your journey of healing. It will also instill a feeling of hope and strength to keep moving forward no matter how bad things are in the moment because you'll know you're slowly building a strong foundation for a more empowering life.

- Spending time in solitude in nature.

Being in nature, heals. The warmth of the sun on your skin, the smell of the earth, sound of birds or water, wind swaying the trees are all great for making your senses come alive and reconnecting you with the flow of life. When in nature, you're in the moment, and there is a sense of experiencing something greater than yourself, which exactly what you need to develop the power and strength to terminate your abusive relationship. As often as you possibly can, take time to be in nature, even if it's just five minutes sitting by a tree in the park.

- Practice Forgiveness.

This is a spiritual practice and trust me, it is easier said than done. When we are the ones being wronged, taken advantage of and abused, practicing forgiveness can be very challenging. But here's the thing, lack of practicing forgiveness only holds you back from experiencing life and keeps you stuck in the very situation you want to escape.

When we hold on to anger, resentment, or a grudge, we waste a lot of energy that could just as well be directed toward creating a life you love. Remaining in the present moment and accepting both pleasure and pain as part of your journey as a human being will enable you to heal and bring back spiritual health and balance sufficiently. The human ego naturally leans toward pleasure and comfort, but if you really want to get at the heart of who you really are, you need to make an effort and discipline yourself more so you can explore all that you are. The real you isn't afraid, or hurt or damaged by pain, and it is this aspect of yourself that you need to reconnect with to overcome the abuse you've faced. When you practice forgiveness (I mean real forgiveness), you open the door and create the space for the real you to emerge. As I said, this won't come easy, and like all practices, it will take time and effort, but you can do it.

This list is far from conclusive, but you have enough here to start practicing and enjoying the benefits of self-care. Start by testing out one or two things from the examples provided. Keep things simple and focus on doing the ones that feel good to you. If what you try doesn't seem to impact you in any way, try something else. The journey of healing after narcissistic abuse is as much a sacred and spiritual journey as it is physical. There is no right or wrong path. The most important thing is that you work on your inner world, find your true self, live from that space, and implement a self-care plan that makes you feel good throughout this process.

Building your immunity and Identity after narcissistic abuse

Many victims and survivors of narcissistic abuse who've grown up under the web of malignant narcissism hardly know that they are suffering from a loss of self-identity. I can recall when it first dawned on me. It was during one of my first internship interviews where I was faced with a situation and couldn't for the life of me figure out what to do because I didn't even know what makes me different. My interviewer asked me what I think makes me different, and I froze. Reflecting on that moment, later on, I realized that I had no sense of identity or value. I honestly didn't think there was anything special about me. Perhaps you've had similar moments in your life?

If so, then you probably feel a lot of resentment and anger (rightfully so), but I am here to encourage you to find a way to let go and move on. It won't happen all at once, but you can heal and rebuild your immunity and self-identity.

The fact that malignant narcissists work on destroying their victim's self-esteem and identity actually proves that they, too, are dealing with their own identity issues. In many cases, your abuser doesn't know who they really are. They have an ideal they are trying to reach, but since they don't know how to do it in a healthy way, they focus on using you and your resources to do it. Similar to how people with substance abuse issues chase after drugs, alcohol, or gambling for that "high," your abuser chases after attention and energy to get their high.

When it comes to reversing the damage and restoring yourself back into full power, understand that it will take time. It is an ongoing process. Just as it didn't happen overnight, healing your self-image and restoring a healthy inner child won't take place at the snap of a finger. But here are a few things to incorporate throughout your recovery to fast track the process.

• Cultivate self-love.

This isn't just about feeling good or taking time for yourself, it's about cultivating a state of appreciation for yourself. Let's face it, we struggle with feeling self-appreciation a lot. Self-love allows you to embrace and even love your weakness along with your strength. It's about having compassion for yourself as you strive to find personal meaning and fulfillment. Ever heard of a concept called Wabi Sabi? Arielle Ford wrote a book called Wabi Sabi Love that extrapolates the ancient Japanese philosophy of Wabi Sabi, which is the acceptance and affectionate regard for imperfection. This is a principle you must practice on yourself until you get tot he point where all you see and feel about yourself is pure unconditional and perfect love.

• Create a strong support structure around your healing.

Part of rebuilding yourself and fully healing is creating boundaries so that others can know how far they can go with you. Where you choose to draw the line between a healthy relationship and a loss of self-identity will determine how your future relationships shape up. If you don't want a repeat of your past, you need to change within and without. Discern between constructive advice and abusive criticism.

• Go after a dream or desire that the narcissist made you believe you can't accomplish.

This could be a lifelong dream that you've always want to turn into reality, a hobby, a career you wanted to pursue or something you've always wanted to experience. Going after the thing your abuser said you couldn't do is a great way to prove to yourself how wrong they are about you, who you are, and what your potential is. Choose to do stuff that makes you come alive and reconnect you with your inner child.

• Take your time and be easy with yourself during this process. No one expects you to figure it all out. At first, it might be tough to even communicate with other people or trust in your own thoughts. It's okay not to know everything about yourself, how things will turn out, or what your future life will look like. This is all part of healing and regaining your real identity. You won't have all the answers, and some days may still be tough to get through. If you put too much pressure on yourself, move too fast, or force things to be what they aren't yet, you risk ending up in another abusive or toxic relationship.

Take your time to heal, recover, and restore your life on your own terms. It may take a few months or a few years. The important thing is that you build a life you love of true freedom.

Chapter 09: No contact

The troubling thought in today's information-driven world is that the Internet contains a lot of stuff that doesn't really get you anywhere.

You've been there, haven't you?

Looking to end the trauma and abuse in your life, and you want to make sure there are no loopholes that will suck you back in. So you go to your trusted friend, Google. You browse through countless articles and videos about narcissistic abuse and before you know it, hours (sometimes days) have gone by, and nothing has been accomplished. In a semi-coma state, you finally give up because the only thing those dozens of blogs have said (aside from ranting on and on about how toxic and demonic narcissists are), is precisely what you already knew. There were no practical steps that could actually help. In fact, the only thing they accomplished was to make you more hysterical and dismayed. You probably needed to pop Xanax just to handle the overload, didn't you?
Well, you're not alone. Many of us try to seek answers on YouTube and blogs but eventually all that negative crap with no real solution causes us to want to give up. I don't want that to be your experience ever again. Here's a practical and straightforward technique to help you gain the sanity and freedom that's been taken from you.

It's a technique known as "No Contact," and I want to share with you exactly what it is, plus how to properly implement and maintain it so that you don't get sucked back into the web of narcissistic abuse.

What No contact is and what it isn't

This is the key that puts an end to the abuse. It locks the malignant narcissist out of your reality and puts an end to their manipulation and shenanigans. We use this technique to make sure the toxic person never again gets access to our emotions, our heart, mind, and spirit.

No contact isn't to be used lightly. It's not meant to be a trick or a game to get your narcissistic abuser interested in you again. Most people confuse No Contact with the silent treatment, so let's clarify that now.

The main difference between silent treatment and No contact is the intention.
Cults, churches, communities, and organizations have used silent treatment, aka cold shoulder, social rejection, isolation, or ostracism for centuries. It is a form of punishment or a way to inflict vengeance for a perceived wrong. The ancient Greeks are famous for using this technique to neutralize someone they considered a threat to the municipal or potential ruler.

In the corporate world, the silent treatment is usually a form of workplace bullying where the managers or supervisors punish the whistle-blower for carrying out unethical behaviors.
In a romantic or family setting, the silent treatment is more like an aggressive measure of control and punishment that narcissists love to use to motivate their victim into a particular behavior. I think silent treatment is the ultimate form of devaluation, and it causes victims to feel alone, neglected, voiceless, and invisible. In short, the silent treatment is a tactic favored by malignant narcissists and is usually used to manipulate you into doing things the way they want. It forces you to shut up and accept whatever crap they want to feed you, and it also allows them to play the hurt victim. No, this isn't anything close to what I want you to do for your healing because the intentions behind true No contact are very different.

With No Contact, you're not attempting to punish or bully anyone. In fact, it's not even about the abuser. This is about you protecting yourself and your reality. No Contact is implemented intentionally, deliberately, and its very nature is to break the cycle of abuse.

It should be used as a way to remove yourself from the influence of the toxic person so you can finally heal and transform your life for the better.
A significant component of healing yourself is being removed from the person and situation that wounds you. And as with all wounds, yours needs ample time to heal without being reinvigorated. By establishing no contact, you remove yourself from being a source of supply in that abusive and dysfunctional relationship.

Why we focus on remaining in No Contact

I know going No Contact is no easy task during the recovery process. However, you must give it your all because it stands as the crux that determines whether you will permanently heal and transform your life or remain a victim forever. The termination of an abusive, dysfunctional relationship usually leaves us feeling dead inside feeling unable to cope. Logically it made sense to terminate that toxic relationship because you know you don't deserve to be mistreated and taken advantage of, but emotions don't deal with logic. When you are madly in love with someone or in the case of having a narcissistic parent as your abuser, it's still hard to completely detach. Your emotions may hijack you and cause you to stray from the path of healing. As I mentioned earlier, while discussing trauma, the "trauma bond" that you form with your abuser will tend to keep you tethered to him or her even though you know it's not right. There's also other factors like feeling undeserving of true love, low self-worth, poor self-image, low self-esteem and co-dependency developed over time can actually keep you falling back into the web of abuse over and over again.

These reasons and so many other variables are the driving motives behind applying the no contact technique. You must create a space for healing, restoring, and rebuilding yourself from the negative influences of your abuser. No contact established the space for you to completely detach from the toxic person and move forward with your life. The more you're "out of touch" with the person both mentally, and physically, the easier it will be to retrain your mind, strengthen and control your emotions. You will be able to objectively look at the situation and relationship without having the malignant narcissist gaslighting you.

The more you practice no contact, the more resilient you become and are more capable of fighting the temptation to fall for the narcissists hoovering and manipulation tactics.

Here's how to apply No Contact immediately

Cut out all interactions and exchanges with the toxic person. That means not personal, virtual, or mental contact. You must remove and block your abuser from your phone, social media network, email, etc. Get rid of all triggers such as photos, gifts, or any other physical reminders that may trigger a memory of them. If the narcissist requests in any way shape or form to meet up immediately decline the offer.

This also means cutting them out mentally, which most victims forget to do. It's great to take physical measures to block the person from your life, but if you're spending most of the day thinking about, conducting conversations and arguments with the person in your head - then you're not practicing No Contact. You also need to avoid that urge to check on their updates through friends, social media, or other indirect ways. My best recommendation if you do have lots of friends in common with the abuser is to cut all contact with them too (at least as much as possible) and instead create a new support network that is separate and far removed from the influence of the malignant narcissist. Following the examples and suggestions I have given on the subject of self-care practices, this should not be too hard to accomplish.

Let's talk about specific examples that you need to exercise your No Contact technique rigorously.

• If your narcissistic abuser made a key to your home without your knowledge and popped in to "check on you," flee the scene immediately. You can absolutely not engage them directly. The best course of action is No contact.

•If the narcissist doesn't have a key but still shows up to your home uninvited, do not answer the door. If they are still hanging around trying to get your attention to consider calling your local authority for help. Maintain no contact at all cost even if they brought a Mariachi band to serenade you.

• If you're walking toward your car from Yoga class or the weekly supermarket run and the narcissist appears from nowhere - make like the wind and drive away as fast as possible. Do not engage them in any conversation even if you want to yell at them for stalking you.

Sticking to your No Contact Rule

If you find yourself struggling to maintain No Contact with your abuser, consider scheduling your week with pleasurable activities that distract you. Get a massage, take long walks, read inspiring books, start a new hobby. Figure out a passion that you'd like to work on and devote as much energy as you can to that passion project. You can also integrate all the self-care tips that I offered. One great way of tracking and maintaining your progress as you implement this technique is to journal your thoughts daily. It can be a private journal, or if you're courageous enough, you can document the entire process as a blog journal. Where and how you do it doesn't really matter; what matters is that you find a safe outlet for your thoughts and emotions so they can stop hindering your progress. As you progress don't forget to celebrate your wins as well no matter how small. Both challenges and successful milestones deserve to be acknowledged as that is the path of healing and full recovery.

When a full No Contact isn't possible, what then?

Sometimes going No Contact just isn't possible. For example, if you have shared custody of the children or a legally binding business contract. In such cases, modified No Contact is the only solution to enforce so you can protect your emotions and allow healing to transpire. For many women divorcing their narcissistic husbands, things get really muddy when they get to this phase of recovery. If proper No Contact isn't carried out and the victim attempts to "stay friends" for the sake of the children she accomplishes many things none of which are healthy or progressive for her well-being.

This became really evident for Sheryl as she shares her story with us.
"I was in a 17-year relationship with my narcissistic abuser, 14 of those we were married. I ignored many red flags from the very beginning of our relationship, but his charm and love bombing were addictive. He caused me to lose not one but two professional careers, refused to move close to my family, and still, I stayed. After he retired, he left me alone for six months to work in a different state and refused to compromise. When he would get angry with me, which happened most of the time, he shouted, pushed me, called me names, slammed doors and would disappear from the house for hours just to punish me. He usually said, 'since you hate

being alone, I'll make sure you stay alone forever.' Finally, I had enough and took some legal action this one time when we pushed me right after I had undergone surgery. But then a little while later he got sick and had to stay in the hospital for a while, so I decided to dissolve the legal action and help him out. He recently filed for divorce, and now I have lots of anxiety around this because I don't know if I can start over as my income is not what it should be. As I deal with the divorce I was trying to find a more amicable way of dealing with things and even suggested separation instead so that I can still keep my health insurance, I can see all it does is feed his already inflated ego. His adamant on getting this divorce and blames all our marital issues on me. I have to admit, I do feel guilty about some of the things I've said to him while angry and I know I keep bringing up the horrible things he's done to me which only makes him more furious but most of all, I wish I had the strength to leave sooner."

From that single example, it's clear to see avoiding No Contact with your abuser only enhances your suffering. It takes away your credibility for any boundaries or requests you make. You'll find yourself falling back when the narcissist needs extra "supply," and once they are done with you, they'll discard you yet again. Unfortunately, this enhances your feelings of self-loathing because you're holding out for a person who will never reciprocate your emotions, affections, or see value in you.

Therefore it goes without saying, No contact is the best solution. But if you can't do a full No contact, modify it with great caution taking extra measures to ensure your abuser is sealed off from your mind, body, and spirit. Remember, it is your birthright and responsibility to be happy, healed, healthy, and enjoy a good life. You don't have to prove to anyone (especially not the narcissist) that you are a good person. Leaving the lines of communication open or entertaining loopholes for them to get back in your head only delays your recovery and healing. Taking these extreme measures to cut all contact will be difficult and may even hurt in the beginning, but if you stick to it and keep forging forward, you will finally create healthy, empowering boundaries for your life that will enable you to thrive in all ways.

Chapter 10: 3 Steps To Reclaiming Your Power

By now, you are more than ready, educated, and equipped to begin your journey to healing and recovery. But there's one more life hack I wish to leave you with. You see, I believe that what we crave more than anything after going through abuse and trauma is to experience a sense of freedom and power. As victims of narcissistic abuse, we need to be able to do what we want, how we want, when we want, and we need to feel loveable again. Even if we remove the source of our pain, it's important we take measures to reignite that sense of freedom and power that was taken from us.

I know what it's like to be silenced, to feel invisible, unworthy, and undermined. That feeling of wanting to crawl into the deepest, darkest hole in the universe and just die there is all too familiar to me, and I know how hard it can be to break free from those old physical and psychological chains. In fact, after years of working on myself, I realize psychological chains are much stronger than physical chains. With everything, we've shared in this book, you now have a clear path to wholeness, truth, and incredible awareness. And there's one more thing you need to do for yourself to anchor yourself fully into the way of recovery.

It's a three-step process that will empower you to gain mastery over your emotions and reclaim personal power. The more of your personal power you can access, the faster and more permanent your recovery will be.

1. Take back your story and rewrite it.

Malignant narcissists are professionals at forcing false narratives on their victims. Unfortunately, we tend to buy into these fake stories and believe in them, which often places the abuser in the position of power. The fact that your narcissistic abuser is always right and you have no authority over what he or she says is a perfect example of this false narrative. As the abuser justifies the abuse, all you can do is affirm their perspective. Gaslighting is one of the ways narcissistic abusers feed their victims with false stories and negative self-perception.

Among the many false perceptions victims usually believe (for example, "you are damaged goods" or "you are not loveable") nothing is more harmful to the recovery process than carrying on the false self-beliefs and negatively charged trauma story.

By keeping the victim story alive and central to your life, you actually make it your whole life story, which continues to keep you in that same cycle. So now that your abuser is out of your life for good, this is your opportunity to rewrite the story of your life so that it can serve you as you rebuild your life. You cannot change the past or the pain you've had to endure, and you certainly cannot change your abuser. What you can change is the emotional charge and interpretation of the experience. I want you to undo the lies and manipulation through your own self-actualization and awakening. This will stretch you and won't necessarily be easy, but you must do it if you want to reclaim your personal power.

This doesn't mean going public with your story or anything that doesn't feel right to you. Instead, I want you to own this part of your life and perceive it as a chapter in your book of life. Whenever you look back at that chapter, I don't want you plunging back into pain and depression. So what are some things you can do to ensure that never happens?

A friend of mine who also grew up with an abusive parent decided to take this step seriously. He sat down one weekend with a journal and wrote down the story of his childhood in a manner that made him feel more empowered. Instead of seeing himself as a victim of abuse, he rewrote that chapter of his life depicting himself as a boy who learned very early in life to strong and independent thanks for the absence of his father. And his dysfunctional relationship with his mother was turned into a lifelong lesson on compassion and the understanding that not all mothers know how to express love in a healthy way. This in no way justified the hurt and trauma he'd experienced, but it did take the sting, resentment, and hatred out of his childhood memories restoring him to full power.

I invite you to reflect on your own trauma and pain. How can you take back your story and rewrite it so that in the coming months, years and decades you can look back with genuine compassion?

2. Forgive yourself.

I said it before, but it bears repeating here that forgiveness is one of the most powerful practices in recovery. Releasing the pain and trauma caused by your narcissistic abuser instead of choosing to hold on to it will help you heal faster. It's not easy, but it is possible to forgive completely. In a study in the Journal of Consulting and Clinical Psychology, Forgiveness Therapy showed the most promise as a way to overcome emotional trauma as compared to other forms of therapies. The control group that was treated using Forgiveness Therapy showed more significant signs of improvement over five years.

I want you to realize that you are not your past experiences, the emotions that usually torment you, and you are certainly not your mistakes. Feelings of guilt and shame must be eliminated from your mind. Acknowledge them when they show up, observe them without judgment, and choose to release them. You are not your thoughts or emotions. It is essential to your healing that you work on forgiving and accepting yourself unconditionally. Evict that internal voice that judges you all the time and instead practice the self-love and self-compassion practices that I shared earlier. The more you do this, the deeper your healing will be.

3. Rebuild your self-image and recognize your true worth.

I can't. I'm a failure. I don't feel worthy. I am weak. I'm unlovable must be replaced with new thought patterns and a new self-image. Repeat out loud right now the following: I can. I am succeeding in life. I am worthy of love and all good things. I am strong and confident. I am loveable. I love myself.

Let these thoughts be your new frame of mind. You must rebuild your self-image from victimhood to victorious. Challenge the inner dialogue and limitations that you notice inside your head. Get curious about your potential, who you really are, why you are here, and what purpose your life serves.

Louise Hay was a famous healer, metaphysical counselor and the founder of Hay House publishing (a company that has grown so much over the years that people like Wayne Dyer and

Deepak Chopra published their books with her). She sold out countless seminars and trainings where she taught people how to do what she called "mirror work". An exercise in self-love where you'd look at yourself and speak words of truth and love until it becomes the new norm. What made Louise Hay so famous aside from her many books on self-healing was her unique story of triumph over devastating childhood trauma. Growing up she had a very dysfunctional childhood, experienced a lot of abuse and spent a big part of her life as a victim. In fact Louise Hay didn't recover and transform her life until she was in her 50s. In one of the recorded tapes that you can easily access on YouTube, she says that the words we speak and the thoughts we think about ourselves have more power than we know. They are the ones that keep us disconnected, stuck and in pain. It's not about what happened to you, it's about what you are doing now and the ideas you hold as true about yourself. There is no type of abuse or trauma you cannot recover from and Louise Hay did a good job proving it so.

Therefore, if you can find a way to tune into that power that lies within you, sustaining you at every moment - life will change for the better. You and I are not responsible for ensuring our bodies do the millions of things they do at each and every moment. I don't even know how my heart beats, and my lungs work, whether I am awake, asleep, angry, happy, or sad. The fact that the sun rises in the morning without fail, and winter always follows fall is a mystery too big to comprehend. We know life is bigger than us and yet we often get bullied into believing that we are helpless when that same power that makes that breathes life into birds and all the creatures of this planet is right here for us. Why not seek to understand how to access that same power that keeps the earth spinning on its own axis? Why not build an image of yourself that feels congruent with the grandeur and magnificence that is life itself? Why settle to be a second-class citizen of this planet when you are made of stars and have more power pumping through your veins than any human being can fathom?

You see the lies you've been fed all your life have caused you to experience this limited and lower version of life. But if you decide to stop accepting that BS and instead rewrite your story with what feels true to your core, you'd start to experience a completely new version of life. You will never outgrow your self-image because that is your perception of yourself. Malignant narcissists prey on their victims because most of the time, the self-image is distorted, and they can easily manipulate it. Now that you are here, it's time to work on forming a healthy self-image that no one can distort. It's time to define identity and value, not based on what people have told you before but because of the knowledge, understanding, and wisdom you've gained about the power that's breathing you. Until you become a child of this universe, people will always succeed in hindering your potential and value. Once you realize that you are powerful and loved beyond measure, then no one will be able to harm you.

Healing from narcissistic abuse is possible, and although it is very complex trauma, you can recover and rebuild your life. As victims of narcissistic abuse, we usually blame ourselves even without realizing it. Please stop it. Take your time with this process, see it more as a marathon than a sprint and go one day at a time if you must, but whatever you do, keep on the path of recovery. Know that being chained to the web of lies, manipulation, and abuse is not your fault. You are not broken and certainly don't need to accept a life of permanent misery. Although the abuse is part of your life's story, it doesn't and shouldn't be your whole story. Each phase of your recovery is essential, so don't skip over or try to shortcut the process. Understand that the journey is just as important as the destination. When times get really tough, that's okay too. Be in the present moment, soothe yourself as much as possible and keep reminding yourself that your new life isn't about striving for perfection; instead, it is about progress. Your healing and transformation starts with one step. Take your first step today, and remember you are not alone.

Educational Resources

• Journal of Brian Behavior and Cognitive Sciences-http://www.imedpub.com/articles/the-cognitive-neuroscience-of-narcissism.php?aid=22149

• NPD test -https://barendspsychology.com/narcissistic-personality-disorder-test/

• The Gift Of Imperfection By Brené Brown - https://www.amazon.com/gp/product/159285849X/ref=dbs_a_def_rwt_bibl_vppi_i2

• Resource for grounding and soothing techniques - https://www.amherst.edu/system/files/media/Grounding%2520and%2520Self%2520Soothing%2520Techniques.pdf

• Louise Hay you can heal your life - https://www.amazon.com/You-Can-Heal-Your-Life/dp/0937611018

Empath

The Practical Survival Guide For Empaths And The Highly Sensitive Person To Thrive In The Modern World

Copyright 2019, Empath, Alexandra Jessen- All rights reserved.

In no way is it legal to reproduce, duplicate, or transmit any part of this document in either electronic means or in printed format. Recording of this publication is strictly prohibited and any storage of this document is not allowed unless with written permission from the author. All rights reserved.

Table of Contents

Chapter 01: Introduction 96

    What This Book Is Not. 98

    What Is An Empath? 99

    Is Empathy and Empath the same thing? 100

    Emerging Scientific Discoveries 101

    The difference between an Empath and a highly sensitive person 103

    Different Types of Empaths 104

    Am I an empath? 111

Chapter 02: The Game Of Energy 113

    Embracing The Empathic Experience 113

    The Painful Struggle Of Emotional Imbalance 114

    The Five Areas Of Active Expression 116

    Harnessing the power of your emotions 118

    How To Stop Being A Human Sponge 120

Chapter 03: Relationships 122

    Empaths and intimacy 124

    How to manifest your dream relationships 124

    Toxic relationships and energy vampires 126

    Protecting yourself from toxic relationships. 128

    Parenting 130

Chapter 04: Work and Career 139

    Recommended Jobs For Empaths. 141

    How to manifest your dream career as an empath. 142

    Tips To Empower Yourself At Work 144

Chapter 05: Empaths and Self Care 147

Adrenal Fatigue, Exhaustion, and Insomnia. Breaking free of the zombie life. 147

Importance of Self Care For An Empath And Highly Sensitive People 149

Finding Your True Self 152

Locating And Healing Your Emotional Triggers 152

Nutrition And Exercise 156

What is your Dosha or Body Type? 159

Tips For Self-Care 160

Chapter 06: Spirituality And Transcending Limitations As An Empath 165

Finding Peace And Freedom 166

Spiritual awakening: The five stages 168

Daily spiritual practices to help you thrive 172

Next Steps 173

Resources 174

Chapter 01: Introduction

Three years into my psychology degree, I couldn't take it anymore. I had to make a drastic decision about my life and where it was headed before I completely lost it!

Monday morning the alarm goes off at 6.20 am and I immediately get sucked into this feeling of dread. It's like a truck ran over me a dozen times during the night. I only had four hours of sleep, which I suppose is some progress from the three hours of sleep over the past three months. I literally feel and look like one of those characters from the walking dead, except much worse.No matter what I tell myself, getting out of bed just feels like punishment. The muscles in my body ache, yet I haven't been to the gym in months. I have this sick feeling in my stomach that feels like the flu, but I know I'm not ill.

In fact, that feeling follows me around everywhere lately, and it seems to be getting worse on Mondays. In my head, I am already wishing the day would be over so I could just crawl under my sheets and cry over my exhausting life.

Going through my day at the campus was becoming more and more unbearable. Sitting in a group with my friends talking over some negative nonsense and school politics, I felt utterly alone and so misunderstood. Yes, school had never been easy for me (especially the socializing part), but somehow my encouraging mother led me to believe it does get better with time. No, mom, it doesn't.

One time a substitute professor came in to give a lecture, and as soon as she was done I was so nauseous I had to rush to the bathroom to barf. It took weeks before people stopped making fun of me for that incident. "You need to toughen up softy, or you'll never make it in life." they mocked.

Now I realize time does nothing to help someone like me. The bouts of depression that have been showing up ever since I hit my teenage years were never going to go away. No matter how hard I tried to escape, I would always circle back to another "winter season." Each time felt worse than the last. My health was all over the place. Some months I'd feel great, some months it was hellish.

I kept gaining and losing weight even when my diet remained the same. And the thought of spending one more year in a class with my insensitive professors who hardly seemed to understand anything about the human behavior (even though they receive accolades on the topic) made me sick to my gut. Something had to change...

That was my state five years ago. Life was tough. No. It was miserable! I was trying to do good by my parents, friends, teachers, and society, but realized I was destroying myself in the process. I was born into a caring family that valued logic and traditional education and was spending all my life proving my worth by pursuing goals that society deemed right.

Fast forward five years later, and I am a new person. I feel resurrected. A rebirth took place, and it's all because I stopped playing in the shadows. I stopped hiding the aspects of me that others struggled to understand. I quit apologizing for being so keenly aware of how everyone around me genuinely feels even when they try to mask their emotions. I started owning my weirdness, and it has paid off significantly. First, I discovered that I wasn't the only one who had this ability to "feel" people, animals, objects, and places in ways that the average individual can't. More on this in a few minutes.

I also discovered those like me (scattered all over the world) are taking a stand on their unique gifts and learned that some scientists are even starting to study us so they can better understand what makes our kind tick. It isn't that we are more "special" than other human beings; we are merely - different.

And when you know you're different, it becomes necessary to start thinking and living differently. Wouldn't you agree?

If you are still reading this and nodding along, that tells me you, and I share certain similarities. Whether you already know about your unique gifts or are starting to question more about who you really are, trust that you've come across this book at the right time.

Regardless of how much struggle and suffering you've experienced in the past or how alone you've felt, I can promise you one thing: You are not alone.

Everything you've gone through has been preparing you to become the person you were meant to be in this lifetime. And the work that lies ahead of you now requires you to step into your power and embrace the real you. The one you probably don't yet fully understand. And that's okay because by the time you're done reading this book, that new you will emerge clear as day and you will finally find the peace and freedom you deserve.

This was my quest a few years ago when my heart had had enough of doing what everyone was doing. It is my intention that this book can offer you the solace and guidance you need to start thriving as the real and powerful you. Now, I know I'm making some big claims here, and I intend to live up to them, as that is part of my mission today. But having said that, I think it's also essential we set the right expectations. I wouldn't want you to have misconceptions about what this book can do for you.

What This Book Is Not.

This isn't going to be one of those books on empaths that makes it okay for you to continue hiding in the shadows. I know most empaths have been led to believe that the best thing they can do is avoid people, protect themselves from outside forces and accept suffering as a way of life. Most teachings on empaths are about finding coping mechanisms. In other words, there's nothing you can do about your current life so just accept things as they as. This is not one of those books. There's plenty of material to support that mindset if that's more your cup of tea, so I recommend you find that type of message elsewhere.

But here's what I can assure you this book can and will do for you if you let it.
You can finally find practical tools, insights, and processes to help you step out of that lifestyle of quiet desperation and suffering. If you've had enough of that shared experience of being fragile and at the mercy of everyone else's "stuff" then you're ready to consume the content in this book and transform your life. Your health, relationships, career and sense of self-worth can finally transform and become what you've always wanted them to be. Wanna know why?

Because the core message of this book is to take you from a coping surviving empath to a thriving one. That means no more settling for being a doormat or a dumping ground for other people. It means no more giving away your power. Most importantly, it means changing your perception about yourself and what it means to go through life as an empath. If that's what you've been seeking, then take a deep breath, relax and allow the transformation to begin.

What Is An Empath?

Although this is still a term being developed (especially when it comes to scientific studies), we can apply the following working definition: An empath is a person who detects, processes and can absorb the emotions and energies that surround them (if they choose to). This can be from other people, the environment and animals. It's a heightened level of sensitivity, empathy, and compassion. An empath can pick up another person's feelings, physical sensations and can even sense someone's spiritual orientation.

We are highly intuitive, sensitive and caring but we are also like shock absorbers with an extremely porous nervous system and hyperactive reflexes. Our experience of pleasure and pain is so intense and can sometimes become overwhelming.

Let me ask you this... Have you spent all your life being told that you're "too sensitive" or that you need to grow thicker skin?

That's all I heard growing up. I would walk into a mall perfectly fine and walk out with aches and pains that came from who knows where! A day at the mall was something I didn't enjoy because I knew it would take me a whole evening (sometimes an entire day) just to recover from the energy drain and strange aches I had picked up. I realized early in my life that being in large crowds or hanging out with certain people exhausted me. And then there was the strange sensation and overload I experienced with bright lights, loud noises, and heavy smells, but I'll share more about that discovery a little later in the book. For now, I want you to see that being an empath is more than just having compassion and caring about others. It is true we approach fellow human beings, animals and our environment different from other people, but it's far more than that. There are certain subtle experiences going on within us, and the more we become aware of what they mean, the better control we can have over our lives.

Many empaths also possess certain natural gifts whether they are aware of it or not and in my experience, much of the restlessness and constriction we tend to feel is because our undeveloped gifts are suffocating within trying to find a way out.

Is Empathy and Empath the same thing?

There is a connection between the two, but they are not one and the same. Empathy is when you are able to put yourself in the shoes of another. It is the ability to understand and share the feelings and thoughts that another is experiencing from his or her point of view. In other words, when you're being empathic, your heart goes out to someone else. You experience deep compassion.

Contemporary researchers are continuing to study this topic and have identified two types of empathy, namely: Affective and Cognitive empathy.
According to the Greater Good Science-based Magazine, "Affective empathy refers to the sensations and feelings we get in response to other's emotion. This can include mirroring what that person is feeling or just feeling stressed when we detect another's fear or anxiety. Cognitive empathy, on the other hand, refers to our ability to identify and understand other people's emotions."

Research is proving that empathy has deep roots in our brains and bodies. It is part of our evolutionary history as human beings, and in fact, we can observe some elementary forms of empathy even in dogs and rats. This leads me to believe that empathy is part of the true nature of every human being. However, there are those that have a more profound experience when it comes to connecting with fellow human beings and nature. We'll talk a bit more about the scientific findings around this topic as the chapters unfold but for now, what I want you to get is that while empathy is a quality inherent in all of us which can be developed and enhanced by those who choose to do so, empaths are individuals who experience more than just empathy and compassion for others.

An empath is capable of absorbing and embodying the feelings of another. I want you to imagine it as a spectrum. On this empathic spectrum, we have on one corner the empath, and as you move toward the middle, you have those that are known as highly sensitive people (we'll talk about that distinction in just a bit). Dr. Elaine Aron has called this group Highly Sensitive People (HSP), but they are not to be confused with empaths. As you move closer to the middle of the empathic spectrum, you'll find people with strong empathy who are not HSPs or empaths. Then as you move further away from the mid-point, toward the opposite side of the spectrum, you'll find sociopaths, psychopaths, and narcissists who are considered to have empath-deficient disorders.

As you can see, on the one extreme we have a person who experiences a heightened version of empathic abilities. Such a person will have a very different encounter going through their daily life and interacting with people. Move further away from that side, and you'll find the average individual who feels some empathy, but it certainly doesn't control their life. To the opposite extreme, you'll find those that have lost any ability to experience compassion. Such a person is considered to be the extreme opposite of the empath (a narcissist), and of course, we'll also talk more about this on the chapter of relationships.

Given the novelty of this topic, science doesn't yet give concrete differentiator between empathy and empaths. But those like me that are empaths can tell you that although empathy is the underlying quality in all of us, those of us who are high on that spectrum also posses other unique attributes that cause us to experience life, relationships and this planet in a different way.

Emerging Scientific Discoveries

Some scientists have been skeptical about whether empaths do really exist. They argue that there is no real evidence to support the claims that we make about our experience of life and others. It is true in the past there has been very little direct evidence, but I see things changing with time thankfully.

Science has proven that we have mirror neurons (a specialized group of cells that are responsible for compassion) in the brain, which are said to enable us to read and understand each other's emotions. For empaths, however, our brain's mirror neuron system is said to be hyperactive. This enables us to absorb other people's energies into our own bodies. The energy may, of course, be positive or negative depending on what we are exposed to.

Other studies used to explain empaths include the concept of emotional contagion which is the idea that when people synchronize, their attitudes, behaviors, and speech they also synchronize their emotions both consciously and unconsciously (Hatfield, Cacioppo & Rapson, 1994). Of course, even such studies don't really do a good job explaining empaths. But in recent years more direct evidence is beginning to be discovered.

Neuroscientist and psychologist Abigail Marsh wrote something intriguing in the book The Fear Factor. She found evidence that there is a difference in the brains of people who are highly empathic to others and called such individuals "altruists." Marsh was motivated to carry out this research based on personal experience, so she wanted to learn what causes people to engage in selfless acts even when there was no direct benefit or when there was a high cost involved. She worked with people who had been involved in the most extreme selfless act that fit into this category. Things like donating kidneys to complete strangers, often anonymously. Sounds like typical empath behavior to me...

Once she recruited the right people, she measured their brain activity while showing them pictures of faces with varying emotional expressions. Then she contrasted this with a control group of people who hadn't performed the same selfless act. For example, she took the people who donated the kidney and showed them varying facial expressions of other people and then showed the same to another control group that did not donate a kidney. The "altruists" were especially sensitive to fearful facial expressions, and when they recognized fear, there was heightened activity in the amygdalae in their brains. Marsh also found that the amygdalae of the "altruists" were 8% larger than those belonging to members of the control group.

Now it is important that I note that Marsh never refers to the altruists as empaths in her book. But if you look at the research, the traits she outlines and the responses she got from this group I believe empaths would be a perfect label. First, she reports that there are different types of altruism, including kin-based, reciprocity-based, and care-based (Marsh, 2016). In her research, she seems to focus more on care-based altruism where no reward or genetic reward to the self is expected. This type of behavior is driven by the concern for the wellbeing of others and nothing more.

Another surprising finding in Marsh's work is how she contrasts psychopaths. Usually, we tend to hear that empaths and psychopaths are polar opposites and Marsh actually refers to the altruist in her study as "anti-psychopaths" because of what her findings showed. When she examined brains of psychopaths the results were the exact opposite of the response garnered from the altruists. The psychopaths were less able to recognize fear on the faces of others and less responsive even when they did. And when it came to the size of their amygdalae, it was 8% smaller than normal.

In other words, psychopaths and altruists both have abnormal brains when it comes to responding to fear and reading facial expressions. The only difference is they are abnormal in opposite directions. This to me appears to support the concept of the empathy spectrum that we usually use. We still have a long way to go when it comes to scientific finding, but this seems like a good start to me. Our experience and intuitive knowing as empaths are starting to receive some scientific backing. It is scientifically accurate that a psychopath will neither feel nor react to the fear of others while those of us who are empaths can't help but feel and move to respond to the fears of others as if they were our own.

The difference between an Empath and a highly sensitive person

Most highly sensitive people would qualify as empaths, but it is not a fact as they are not mutually exclusive. Both empaths and highly sensitive people share similar qualities such as the need for alone time, and high sensory sensitivity which means they are both super sensitive to sound, smell and light. Both have a low threshold for stimulation and in fact, takes them longer to wind down after a busy day. Highly sensitive people are usually introverts, but you can find both introverts and extroverts with empaths. Both share a deep connection and love of nature and always prefer quiet environments.

One of the core differences, however, is that as empaths we can take the experience of energy and emotions much further. We can sense very subtle energy, and we can absorb these energies from other people and the environment. Due to our ability to absorb into our bodies the energy around us, we sometimes have a hard time telling it apart from our own. And if the other person is experiencing pain, discomfort, joy or hurt, we can experience that same energy as if it were our own. This isn't something that a highly sensitive person would go through.

Again, let's go back to that imaginary empathic spectrum I spoke about, an empath would be at the far end (the extreme corner) of the spectrum whereas the highly sensitive person would be further in, closer to the middle of the spectrum where people with strong empathy reside.

Studies have shown that about fifteen to twenty percent of the population in the United States of America alone is comprised of highly sensitive people. Although it is related to being an introvert, there's more to it than that. For example, if you realize that you get easily overwhelmed when you have a lot to do or that you don't perform well in noisy environments and can't stand violent media, then it's very possible you are a highly sensitive person.

Being a highly sensitive person or an empath doesn't mean there's something wrong with you. It's certainly nothing to be ashamed of. You simply process information and data more deeply, and it's essential you recognize this so you can make adjustments in your lifestyle and work environment. Whether you are both an empath and a highly sensitive person or feel like you're only a highly sensitive person, this book will empower you with tools and practices that will help you thrive in all areas of life that matter to you so keep reading.

Different Types of Empaths

With empaths, you best believe there are varying types mostly depending on the personality type as well as the gifts they possess. But let's pause for a moment before jumping into categorization and allow me to share with you the main difference that exists within the empath community.
I firmly believe the main difference that is worthy of serious discussion is whether one is an empowered or disempowered empath.

An empowered empath:

This is an empath who is self-aware, knows his or her sensitivities, special talents and has learned to handle them positively. Such a person has developed his or her mental, emotional, physical and spiritual aspects and lives from a place of power. Being an empath is a gift, and they go through life on purpose, shining their light, thriving and making a difference in this world through these gifts.

When it comes to detecting and processing emotions and energy in their surrounding, they are masters. They not only do it without compromising their own state, they even know how to influence the energy around them and can often perform healing sessions quite effortlessly. To illustrate this type of empath, imagine yourself being an empowered empath walking into a room where friends are sitting exchanging the latest gossip. One of your friends isn't feeling too well. You immediately pick up on the negative vibes and process the information coming in as unwanted, so you dissolve that energy pattern and radiate outward more soothing energy. Although you choose to leave that gathering because you realize it won't be beneficial for you, the energy that you leave them with makes them say " I always feel so much better when you are around. I wish you could stay longer."

When you're an empowered empath, you have the power to influence the energy around you and help others feel better without getting caught up in their negative vibes.

A disempowered empath:

As you might have guessed, this is an empath who is still in the struggle and suffering phase. While they may know of their empathic abilities and special sensitivities, they certainly haven't developed themselves. Such a person feels powerless, at the mercy of others and probably hasn't found a way to make good use of their powers. Being an empath feels more like a curse and dealing with daily human living is a constant struggle. When it comes to detecting and processing emotions around them, they feel very fragile and incapable of controlling anything.

This is why you'll hear many people say empaths are emotional sponges at the mercy of energy vampires.

To illustrate this type of empath, all you have to do is type in the term on Google, and you'll find all kinds of examples. And even if I were to contrast from the empowered empath illustration, walking into a room with that same group of friends sending off that negative vibe would be a common occurrence and you'd probably find your mood changing, body aching and energy drained soon after hanging out with them. This is the information so many books, teachers and blogs leave out.

They are so focused on the suffering and struggles of being empaths they forget to mention that one always has the power of choice. You can choose whether to live your life as a disempowered or an empowered empath. If you can gain clarity on these two main differences, the rest of the book will carry many useful lessons and eye-openers that will enable you to step into a life you love living as an empath.

Now, let's get back to discussing the different categories that have been created within the empath community. Just know that things often get really complicated when trying to identify all the varieties of empaths that exist and I bet there are many more we are yet to uncover. But there is a main "umbrella" that covers all the different types with their unique gifts. This can be categorized into two: Introverted empaths (the majority within the empath group) and extroverted empaths.

Introverted and extroverted empaths might share similarities and even possess some of the same gifts, but their personalities will vary. And depending on which you are, your needs and how you recharge will be different. For example, I am an introverted empath. I love being on my own, connecting with my own energy and nature. I love space and solitude. My way of refueling and recharging requires me to be on my own. Large crowdy places, big parties with lots of people are not a preference. I would rather have one on one interactions or small intimate groups. I need to be close to the water as much as possible.

I have a friend who is also an empath, but she's an example of an extroverted empath. She loves parties and doing dinner dates. I call her a social bird, and it really does suit her because whether she's at work, in the supermarket, at Starbucks or lining up at the bank, she's the girl always smiling and looking to start a conversation. Her way of refueling doesn't actually need time alone (like me). She is a deep sleeper and requires around ten hours of deep sleep, which is where she believes her refueling happens. So as you can see we are both empaths but certainly different in the way we express it and in how we relate to the world around us. Bottom line is that this will vary from one empath to the next depending on how he or she processes sensations, information, and energy.

Aside from that core personality based difference within empaths we also possess certain gifts that each of us were born with. These are talents hidden deep within us, and it is our job to uncover, develop and share these talents with the world. Sometimes, due to traumatic childhood experiences, our abilities get muted out, and we struggle to reconnect with that aspect of ourselves. I believe many empaths struggle with anxiety, low self-esteem, and reclusion because there's a disconnect between who they are authentically and the false conditioning that has become their daily life. When you learn to hide from the world all your life, that inner restlessness will always haunt you, but it's hard to pinpoint where it's coming from. That was part of my struggle as well so if you're having a hard time feeling like you are valuable, please be easy on yourself. It's a phase we all have to go through boldly, and the best way to do it is by becoming aware of your talent, developing it, turning it into a useful skill and courageously sharing it with the world. I'm going to be sharing with you an example of a girl who did just that and turned her negative situation into a six-figure business. I do it not to impress you with the idea of financial gain but because I want to impress upon you the importance of owning the talents that come naturally to you. The light that you shine in this world deserves to be known, and it was meant to be used in service to others.

This is why I want us to dive deeper into the different qualities and talents an empath might have. It is important to mention here that having talent is one thing, turning it into a skill is another. Your ability to earn a good living doing something you love and helping people out with whatever gift you possess depends on you developing your talent into an active skill. Although we are all diverse as empaths, the one thing we all have in common is each one of us comes with certain unique gifts. Find your gift, nurture it, develop it and share it generously in the world. Here are a few talents many empaths find themselves in possession of.

Spiritual Empath

A spiritual empath has direct connections to other realms. Most people refer to these types of empaths as mediums. They usually possess the ability to connect with spiritual beings from other realms, deceased human beings, and other spirits. They also tend to possess psychic empathic abilities that include being able to feel physical and emotional symptoms from their communication with the spiritual realm. It's similar to how an emotional empath can connect and sense with those in the physical realm, this empath connects with others in the spiritual world.

Earth Empath

This type of an empath is connected to the earth in a more than ordinary way. He or she can intuit the earth's changes consciously and at a very cellular level. If you are this type of an empath, then your experience of nature is anything but mundane. You can feel the power of the thunderstorm, and the warmth of the sun rests on your shoulders. The beauty and health of the earth nourishes and refuels you. The moon, the ocean, and tides affect everyone but especially you. The beauty and magnificence of a waterfall exhilarate you whereas air pollutants make you feel ill, exhausted and depressed. You are also sensitive to weather changes and the amount of daylight. As an earth empath, you are prone to Seasonal Affective Disorders (SAD), which makes you fall into depression or "catch the blues" during winter when days are shorter.

Physical empath

If you are a physical empath, then you've probably noticed that you can feel someone else's pain or anxiety in your body and that you usually have so many unexplained symptoms. You're chronically tired, and every time you see a doctor, the response is always the same. "You're fine, just get more rest." But you know something isn't quite right no matter what the doctors say. Empaths who are so porous and can't help but pick up other people's symptoms are what we call physical empaths. And I can tell you, this one is really tricky because you need to be very mindful and in control of your whole self whenever you're dealing with other people.

Otherwise, you might walk into a restaurant for dinner with a new boyfriend and leave with a cold or fever even before dessert!

My friend Jenny recently had this experience, and it was the worst. She had been excited to go on a first date with this new guy for about three months and even bought a particular "black dress" for the occasion. On the afternoon of the date when I saw her, she was perfectly healthy. By the time she called me later that night she was struggling to cure a fever that somehow took over right in the middle of her date. Ouch! As you can imagine, the night didn't go as perfectly as she had planned. In retracing her steps, she quickly realized she had paid close attention to a woman sitting near her table who didn't "feel" well or happy to Jenny. The woman was trying really hard to get through the night, but Jenny sensed her discomfort and anxiousness. It also seemed as though she was experiencing a terrible migraine and kept ordering more ice. Unfortunately for Jenny, she started experiencing the same in her body, and before she knew it, her palms were sweaty, she couldn't breathe so well, and they had to leave.

For some physical empaths things can get so bad they end up being ill for years. Dealing with big crowds, other people's stress, anger and pain can drain them a lot. Physical empaths (who are not yet empowered and in control of their sensitivities) do not have the defenses that others have to screen or filter things out, and that's why it's so crucial to self-check to see if you are one. Trust me, this can be a revelation that changes everything in your world, it certainly changed mine. If you do identify with this type of empath, trust me you are not crazy, there's nothing wrong with you, and you are definitely not a hypochondriac or malingerer. What you are is a really sensitive and gifted empath. The more you learn how to manage, protect and harness your unique way of being the more you can thrive.

Psychometric Empath

This type of empath has a unique ability to receive energy, memories and significant information from physical objects. This can be clothing, photographs, jewelry or any other type of physical object. If you realize that when you touch or come into contact with a physical object some new information streams into your consciousness, then you could very well be a psychometric empath. The more you develop this into a skill, the more powerful it becomes. You can also detect if there is any "dark" presence or energy in things.

Precognitive Empath

This type of empath has the power to receive visions about the future and can foretell an upcoming event. He or she can glance at something that isn't yet manifested and predict it accurately. If this is one of your unique abilities, then you've probably experienced events in your dreams, which then come to pass. Usually, your information is passed on while you dream or meditate. You can either receive signals relevant to some future events or see exactly what's going to happen.

Geomantic empath

A geomantic empath also called an environmental empath has the ability to connect to the physical landscape of a place. If you are this type of empath, then you've probably found yourself feeling unhappy or uncomfortable in certain places, and you couldn't logically explain why. On the contrast, you might feel drawn to certain places and experience a deep connection to places you've never even been to before. You also tend to be attracted to churches, sacred stones, groves or other areas of divine power. It's easy for you to pick up on the energy of a place or location and can be able to sense joy, fear sadness or any other dormant energetic presence that a place has. Similar to earth empath, you feel a powerful connection to the natural world and being out in nature is the best way for you to recharge. Developing this natural connection to the natural surroundings around you could lead to very intriguing opportunities so do your best to connect more with this aspect of yourself and surround yourself with natural materials as much as possible.

Animal Empath

An animal empath has a special connection with animals. He or she can feel what it's like to be that animal and one can even observe a particular communication or exchange happening between the empath and the animal. If this is you, then you'll notice that animals are very drawn to you. As you learn to develop this gift, you'll be able to help pets and their owners, and it won't be too hard to make a killer living working with animals.

For example, I read a story on Facebook of a girl who was sharing how she's managed to create a six-figure business just from dog walking. Well, it first started as a dog-walking job. She needed to make money fast after completing her degree but was struggling to find work and pay off student loans. Then someone recommended she offer some dog walking services around the neighborhood since everyone knew how much pets loved her. Within three months of starting she was already overbooked. Then she had the brilliant idea of leveraging her newly acquired design skills to create animal accessories and sell them to her clients and via Facebook. Three years in and her business is now making six figures in annual revenue. Talk about sharing your light with the world. She's happy, doing what she loves and making a lot of animals really happy. I even read a testimonial of an old lady that said she hires this girl to accompany them to the vet because her dog is always more calm and receptive to the doctor when the dog sitter is around. Booking her for such things now costs hundreds of dollars, which the dog owners consider money well spent. That's the power of using your light to design a life you love living.

Am I an empath?

If you've been questioning whether or not you are an empath, especially since you found out there is such a thing, the best way to get answers is through self-reflection. By taking the time to go within and ask yourself a few questions, you'll be able to tell whether there's resonance with the attributes and traits that most empaths possess.

I am sure you're highly intuitive; as such I trust you'll allow this process to be as natural and resistance free as possible. When something feels right and true for you, it probably is. When it doesn't, then don't force yourself to fit in just for the sake of it. You might find that some of the questions I share below don't resonate and that's okay.

It's also possible to find other teachers saying empaths are introverted and perhaps you are social and extroverted. That doesn't mean you're not an empath, it just means you are unique. As a one of a kind human being, trying to fit into one perfect category is still falling short of expressing who you really are. Therefore regardless of how well you identify with these standard questions, know that you will most likely express your empathic abilities in your own uncommon way. Answer the following questions inspired by Dr. Judith Orloff's self-assessment test. If you strongly agree the answer will be yes. Strongly disagree with a no.

1. When you walk into a room, you can always pick up the "energy" or vibe of the place.
2. You always tell very quickly if someone says one thing but means another.
3. Your mood shifts depending on who walks into the room.
4. Large crowds usually overwhelm you.
5. You feel drained after being around certain people for too long.
6. Being around certain people makes you feel sick.
7. You often feel the pain or discomfort of other people and animals.
8. People usually come to you when they have a problem.
9. The energy of the ocean, forest, mountain or nature, in general, is preferable to the city.
10. You have to be near water.
11. Violent media is a huge turn off for you because you get physically or emotionally ill when exposed to it.
12. You notice you can influence the moods of those around you.
13. Often you can't tell if you're feeling your own emotions or someone else's.
14. Anxiety and overwhelm are common occurrences for you.
15. Multitasking or taking on too much at once is an energy drainer, and you prefer to do one thing at a time.
16. You prefer one-to-one interactions or small intimate groups but certainly not large gatherings.
17. Intimate relationships are great, but you worry they will suffocate you.
18. You often feel like you don't "fit in."
19. Yelling, conflict, and fighting make you sick.

The more agreement you make with these statements, the more you would be considered a full-blown empath. If you responded yes to at least five of these statements, then we would consider you partially an empath.

Answering yes to fifty percent of these statements means you have strong empathic tendencies and of course if you answer yes to over sixty percent then welcome to the world of living as a full-blown empath. In the following chapters, I show you how to get empowered and thrive.

Chapter 02: The Game Of Energy

One of the biggest revelations this book can give you is that of recognizing that you are playing the game of energy. Everything around us vibrates, and we as empaths have naturally been gifted with the ability to sense those vibrations and even embody them. So when we recognize an energy pattern in or around us that doesn't empower and uplift us, it is our duty to quickly dissolve and transform that energy first within our bodies and if possible extend it outwardly to others as well.

I believe empaths have the power to bring about healing and high frequency energies that can literally heal people, animals, and our planet. But we cannot give what we have not got so before we talk about using our gifts and powers to help others we must first master helping ourselves.

Embracing The Empathic Experience

Most empaths confess that they just don't feel like they fit in. They go their whole lives trying to blend in and stay under the radar, even as their emotional discomfort and restlessness continue to pile on. For many empaths, their unique abilities and sensitivities go unappreciated. This is true by normal societal measures because we live on a planet that is very focused on competition, material accomplishments, getting ahead, resenting each other and so on. This is a very different perspective from the one held by an empath. If we grow up in an environment that doesn't embrace our uniqueness then often a conflict emerges within us because we constantly feel lost, misunderstood and unappreciated. The burden of having to carry around our unresolved conflicts as well as the sensitivity to other people's emotions (whether they are aware of their own emotions or not) can be a daunting task, and I think that's where many of us struggle. Coping with daily life as an empath in a world that is insensitive is not easy. Trying to explain to someone who has lost touch with their own emotions what it's like to be me is almost impossible. They will call me strange, abnormal, weird and weak. If I make the mistake (which I did in the past) of believing their opinion, then I imprison myself falsely, and life becomes almost unbearable.

I read an article on the Internet shared by an empath called Zoey who was confessing how tough things have been for her over the past twenty-six years. She recently discovered that she's an empath and that there are many of us in the world which finally gave her the peace and sense of belonging she's been searching for. "I used to dream about shapes and music, and the feelings that went along with different shapes. Trying to explain the color green to a non-empath is a lot easier than trying to explain what a shape feels like. Trust me, not only do they think you're extremely odd, but someone once asked me if I smoke an illegal substance."

There are many more who could share similar frustrations as they try to fit in where they don't. The only path of freedom for us as empaths is to step into our power, recognize that it's not about fitting into society. It's about mastering the unique gifts we bring to the table and gathering more with those that get us. The way we feel, see, experience and express ourselves is different and that's not something to be ashamed of. Who you are is what you need to learn to celebrate and boldly demonstrate in the world. Your job now is to find your truth and unique abilities and live that truth. Use your unique gifts and skills to bring to life the conditions and experiences that you've always dreamed of. The more you do, the more impactful and enjoyable your life becomes.

The Painful Struggle Of Emotional Imbalance

Before your life can go from burdensome, constricting and draining to magnificent, you'll have to come to grips with the same truth I had to face. Nothing changes unless you change first.

The main change you'll have to make is taking full ownership of your energy and learning to distinguish when you're experiencing your own emotions and when it is that of another. Discord within you is an indicator that something is out of whack and everything will continue to be a painful struggle unless you learn to replace emotional discord with harmony. You must gain mastery over your emotions and learn to handle your sensitivities. This is the difference between empowered empaths and disempowered empaths. The way to move from victimhood and feeling like this is a curse begins with a conscious decision. Choose to work on understanding your emotions and abilities.

Chances are you go through life feeling like the weight of the world is on your shoulders. You see the depths of the world's problems and feel the hurt, pain, and confusion that's being caused by greed, injustice, and war. You're also keenly aware of the heavy stuff that people tend to dump on you whenever they turn to you for relief from their issues. There's no way around this. I'm not going to tell you that it's easy living in our current world as an empath. But just because it's challenging doesn't mean it should be unbearable. There are two choices you have once you discover that you are an empath. The first choice is carrying on as you were - feeling the angst, discord, and stress of having these abilities. This is the victim state. Feeling sorry for yourself, wondering why this is happening to you and hating your life doesn't change the fact that you are still alive and walking this human journey. You will continue to create conditions and life experience even if you choose to spend the rest of your days in bed under covers. The second choice you have is to reap the benefits of having these abilities. It's about stepping into your power and learning to make empathy work for you, so you don't become a victim to other people's emotions and thought processes. It's also about learning to take care of yourself more and putting your needs first. That's a tough one for empaths, I know. And I've devoted a section on self-care tips that I'm sure will help you a lot.

Once you decide to become an empowered empath, the next step in ending the struggle and suffering is to understand what emotions are and how they help shape your reality.

So what are emotions?

An emotion is a thought linked to a sensation. A thought is in the mind, and the sensation is in the body, that's why we call our emotions feelings. The mind is an embodied (in the body) and relational process that regulates the flow of energy and information in our body. I learned this definition from Deepak Chopra, and it has served me well over the years because it gives me a scientific and practical way of understanding what my emotions are and how they affect and shape my reality. It also helps me realize that the bigger game I am playing as a gifted empath is that of Energy. Learning how to harness, read, sense and transmute energy into anything I desire better than most.

Dr. Chopra also teaches that there are two basic types of emotions. Emotions that connect us to life. They include love, kindness, joy, compassion, gratitude, and equanimity. Then there are emotions that alienate us from life. They include fear, resentment, hostility, greed, jealousy, anger, guilt, shame, and depression. All these emotions are mediated by the part of our brain called the limbic system. All self-regulation and what is known as homeostasis takes place in this part of our brain. Since we now realize that the limbic brain is also the seat of emotions, our experience of life and whether we create an experience of great joy or great suffering will depend greatly on whether we dwell on negative emotions or positive ones. Peace and harmony in your outer world is, therefore, a direct expression of your inner emotional state. Now, for most people, creating a relatively calm internal state is easier since they don't go around receiving all the surrounding energies. But for empaths, it takes a conscious effort on our part to maintain control of our inner state. In other words, if we are so exposed to an insensitive, greedy, hate-filled and fearful environment, we tend to soak up more of that frequency which only devastates our well-being and state of mind. As a result, we shape our reality accordingly and end up struggling, suffering from depression anxiety and so on. The more aware we become of who we are, how our mind works and the energies we entertain in our inner world, the more power we'll have to end struggle and imbalance within. Over time, we are then able to not only create inner harmony, but we can also influence our immediate surrounding and others.

Are you starting to see the tremendous power you possess as an empath?

The Five Areas Of Active Expression

We have just discovered that your outer world is a reflection of your inner world. When this first hit me, all I wanted to do is start fixing some of the areas that were not working for me. Mainly my relationships, health, and finances. Can you relate?

If you've been feeling stuck lately and you believe you'll never find a way out, the negative emotions associated with your beliefs will reinforce the way you see yourself in the world, and every area of your life shall reflect the same. There are five main areas that I think empaths really need help with. Health, relationships, finances, spiritual, and career. By properly utilizing the gifts we've been given we can actually use our emotions to inform and enhance these four areas rather than hinder them. So here's a simple solution to experiment with right now.

1. Take a private journal and write down what you would love to experience and have as your daily reality in each of these areas.

Health.

Finances.

Relationships.

Career/business.

Spiritual growth.

Make sure each section gets a full page where you describe with as much color as you can the future conditions that you wish to manifest.

2. Now contrast that with where you are and notice how you interpret your current experiences. One of the biggest stumbling blocks we face is that there's so much negatively charged energy in the atmosphere, we tend to pick up on the negatives first. Some psychologists say this is due to our programming while others will say it's just because we are hanging out with the wrong people. Regardless of origin, choose to change your perception about your life, your capabilities, and your potential. Interpretations are your way of assigning meaning to the events and experiences in your life. This is how you "make meaning" out of the things that are happening to you. Empowering interpretations will help you discover the lessons or blessings in every situation, and they will enable you to move forward in life. Empowering interpretations position you to become an empowered empath. As you may have guessed, disempowering interpretations do the opposite. They will cause you to repeat that same cycle of victimhood and being taken advantage of.

In truth, none of the interpretations you choose are any more or less real than another. Your interpretation of your life and who you are is very real to you, and you always have the power to choose the meanings you assign to your circumstances and experiences in life. You may want to interpret the last few years of your life as a curse or a blessing. You may choose to see the progress you're making in reaching your goals, or you can label yourself a failure. The relationships in your life whether positive or negative can either be helping you become a better version of yourself or a severe source of pain. I encourage you to start viewing yourself as a gifted and powerful individual. Someone with untapped potential that's seeking expression in the physical world. The more you choose to focus on how you can create the love life, career, health, family life, and fulfillment you desire instead of focusing on why it can't be, the more positivity you'll begin to experience.

Now that you know what you want in all the areas of your life that matter to you, let's share a few tips on how you can harness the power of your emotions and your unique abilities.

Harnessing the power of your emotions

Did you know that it is just as essential to process your emotions as it is to process the food you eat? We are always picking up on other people's feelings and oftentimes we just blindly absorb and let these emotions camp in our bodies. When we fail to process emotions and experiences, we create toxins similar to the way a body produces toxins, which lead to illnesses when it doesn't process food properly. But the kind of toxins we create are emotional. Anxiety, rage, guilt, sadness, hopelessness, depression and so on are all manifestations of emotional toxins. Over time, if left unchecked they morph into physical symptoms and ultimately become diseases. Having come this far into the book, it's time we start equipping you with some ways of harnessing your healthy emotions so you can slowly learn to maintain inner harmony regardless of the emotions you get exposed to.

• Take responsibility for your feelings. The most important thing you need to recognize at this point is that you have control over your emotions and sensitivities. Disempowered empaths end up being victims in life because they don't feel like they have control over their unique gifts or the emotions that dominate their lives. But the truth is, you always have the power of choice. And with this comes the ability to determine how you will respond or react at any given moment. There is nothing wrong with picking up on someone's negative energy or even landing on your own negative tendencies. Where trouble blooms is when you accept, embody and dwell in that negativity. The first step to thriving as an empath is to take complete ownership of what you feel and the gifts you've been given.

• Deal with emotions as they come up.

Since you are naturally going to pick up on the energy around you, it's best to get into the habit of discerning the emotions that dominate your day and deal with them as soon as they show up. Identify the feeling that you're experiencing, do some breath work to bring yourself more into the present moment, and then name it to tame it. Are you feeling sad, anxious, resentful, overwhelmed, jealous? Where in your body are you feeling this emotion? Ask yourself if these feelings are yours, if they've been triggered by something or if they belong to someone else? Try to figure out why you're reacting in this way and question if there is a better way to react? This doesn't mean you judge yourself. I want you to become your very own private investigator so you can start to understand your triggers.

As you do your breathing and answer these questions, pay attention to the physical manifestation in your body especially where you're experiencing the most discomfort. Keep doing this until you notice the discomfort dissolving.

- Learn to discern when it's your emotions and when it's someone else's.

If you realized that you were reacting to someone else's energetic frequency, collect those emotions into one area and see them dissolving and flowing out from you. Refuse to be a dumping place for other people's unresolved emotions.

- Be process-oriented rather than goal oriented. As empaths, we play to a different tune. That's why most of the commonly preached personal development stuff does very little to help us thrive. Instead of chasing after goals and holding yourself to rigid standards, focus on growing, learning, thriving and showing up as your best self. Give yourself the necessary time and space to create a life you love living. As you move toward your vision, embrace the process. Take note of the day-to-day changes as you progress. Be more mindful of triggers that set you off and respect your sensitivities. Celebrate yourself and this journey even if you're not going at the same pace as others because your journey is unique and no one can tell you what success should look like. Take the time to redefine what some of these labels mean to you in a way that empowers you.

How To Stop Being A Human Sponge

Finding the balance between exercising your empathic abilities and controlling the energies and emotions you pick from others is not an easy task. It's not uncommon for other people's vibes to have an impact on your energy level, emotional state and therefore your life experience. This goes for both good and bad vibes. The more you're surrounded by high-frequency individuals, the more those vibes influence your own reality, and the same is true if you're surrounded by low-frequency individuals. Here's the thing, I haven't yet found a magical single bullet that I can give you to help solve this issue. I also don't have a magic armor that you can wear which can make you instantly impermeable to other people's negativity. But having walked this path I have found a few tips that have gradually helped me develop the skill of being able to filter out, block or instantly process emotions that are detrimental to me.

In other words, I stopped trying to fight my powers, and I stopped judging myself for being so perceptible and sensitive to my environment. Instead, I've learned to embrace all that I am and strengthen myself so that I know the right time to take in and the right time not to. And during those times when I get hit with people's stuff, and I'm completely unprepared, I also know how to process those turbulent emotions, so I don't end up drained and unwell. Here's a fast way of processing negative vibes when they unexpectedly hit.

• Ground yourself.
• Create some distance between you and the negative energy. Whether physically or mentally depending on the situation.
• Personal discernment. Figure out if it's you being triggered. Maybe it's something within you that the other person is triggering. If it is, take note and work on it once you're out of that situation.
• Practice tuning out especially when in the presence of energy vampires.
• Find a technique that works for you that helps you rejuvenate and clears your energy. I like using music because it quickly sends me to my happy place so I can instantly shift back to high vibes before continuing with the rest of my day. Some people prefer praying, meditating or lighting incense. Pick whatever works for you. The main thing is being able to notice what's happening within you and taking quick action before it escalates into something big.

There are more techniques and practices that I will be sharing in upcoming chapters but keep these quick tips as your go-to hacks whenever you need fast relief.

Chapter 03: Relationships

In the previous chapter, I made you aware of the fact that this is a game of energy and self-mastery. To thrive as empaths in today's world, we need awareness about who we truly are and how to make the most of the unique abilities we possess.

In relationships, this becomes all the more important because where two people are exchanging energy, things can get quite constricting and draining for an empath even when that's not the main intention. Your highly sensitive nature and ability to pick up on the energetic frequencies surrounding you makes every relationship quite challenging whether it is romantic, familial or work-related. The closer you connect with someone, the more vulnerable you are to the emotions they radiate and the more you can feel what they are going through mentally, emotionally and physically. If you already work as a healer or during times when you are engaged in sexual intercourse with a partner you know how vulnerable those moments are for you because the energy of another fully penetrates and blends with your own. It is due to this fact that many empaths including myself find handling relationships a very challenging task. We love being affectionate, offering our support, giving of ourselves wholeheartedly but we also know how overwhelming and constricting that constant giving can be.

I struggled to stay in a long-term relationship for most of my adult life because I would always feel in bondage to my partner after a while even if I loved them. Interacting with the same person so much would cause me to feel suffocated and exhausted because I didn't feel like I was getting enough quiet and alone time to replenish my energy. There is a deep desire within me to be alone that constantly battles with my strong passion for love, and although I cannot say I've completely resolved it, I have found a way to create some harmony. Many of the tips I use to create thriving relationships I share in this chapter. Since I know some empaths are also raising children, I have also dedicated a small section of this chapter to discussing how we can manifest better relationships with our children. I'm going to share with you a few lessons I've learned about being an empath in an intimate relationship and how to make it work especially if it's with a non-empath. But before we get there, something I want to address is the struggle and suffering that most of us face.

Why you've struggled, suffered from loneliness and felt misunderstood all your life.

Here's the thing no one wants to talk about. No "right lover" will come into your life and make everything perfect in your world. If you have unresolved issues, wounds that need healing and emotional turbulence, it doesn't really matter who walks into your life, you still won't experience your happily ever after. As long as you're stuck in the frequency of suffering and loneliness, everything you experience will continue to match that frequency. You'll be more prone to attracting people that only solidify that reality. It is easy to become embroiled in an unhealthy and dysfunctional relationship with someone who has strong traits associated with narcissism when one is stuck in a state of struggle and suffering.

Another blind spot we tend to have comes from our natural healing abilities. We get drawn to people who are emotionally wounded and struggling, and those in need of healing of some kind are also drawn to us, but usually, such relationships typically don't end well. This is where codependency comes in. If you are in a relationship with someone who depends on you to heal their wounds or validate them you also unknowingly attach a feeling of worthiness to that person because you know they depend on you for survival.

Being overly invested in the well being of someone you love can lead to great suffering, and it's essential you become aware of the blind spots you have. The intention you need to have as you approach any relationship is to find that overlap between being your best self and loving someone else.

Do any of these experiences ring true for you?
• Arguments make me ill or sick.
• I have difficulty setting boundaries and asserting my needs.
• I absorb my partner's stress, symptoms, and emotions.
• I'm afraid of losing my own identity in a relationship.
• I need to be along to refuel and recharge.

Empaths and intimacy

Intimacy is a big one for us. This is true whether you are dating a fellow empath or a non-empath. We are known as passionate human beings and for a good reason. Our experience of everything is usually pretty intense. We feel everything and everyone, and when it comes to loving someone, we love hard. During the "honeymoon" phase when you just start dating someone things are incredible. It's only as you get deeper into each other, spend more time and open yourself up fully (all the time) to your partner that things start going awry for you. Intimacy in relationships can be fun for you too especially as you learn to step into your full power, manage your sensitivities and attract only the ideal relationships.

Being loved by an empath is one of the most wonderful experience for anyone to go through. However, not many people are prepared for this kind of intense relationship. The contrast of going from intense togetherness to complete space and time alone is a bit of a conundrum and takes a certain type of mindset to fully comprehend why being together and being apart is equally important. And it is that kind of person you should focus on attracting into your life. But you can only attract someone new if you become someone new.

How to manifest your dream relationships

I said it in the last statement. If you want to manifest relationships that nourish and excite you, there must be a fundamental shift in you first. I once read a quote somewhere of a conversation between a father and son. The son asked his father, " How do I find the right woman?" The father replied, "don't worry about finding the right woman just focus on becoming the right man."

It's the perfect mindset for you and me to carry into our lives as well. When I stopped looking for the perfect soul mate and instead placed all my attention of healing my energy, taking control of my emotions, grounding myself and becoming the best version of myself that I could be, that's when things took a major turn in my life. Here's the tough pill you need to swallow. You won't find your ideal soul mate until you become a perfect match for him or her. So what does an ideal relationship entail?

It's about physical attraction and strong natural chemistry.

When you're with your soul mate you feel a shared mutual love and connection, you're comfortable and safe.

It's about being each other's biggest fans and becoming emotional mirrors and teachers.

Your soul mate will "get you," and whenever conflict arises, you will be able to work through them and relinquish unhealthy patterns to improve the relationship.

What it doesn't entail is the following:
One-sided. Meaning it's all about you or all about your partner.
It's also not just a superficial physical attraction where only the sex is good.

A soulful relationship doesn't include abuse, control, rigidity or taking advantage of each other in any way.

It's also not about convenience or just settling down out of fear of being alone. Sometimes a soul mate relationship lasts a lifetime, other times they don't, but regardless, these relationships are transformative and always teach us a lot.

I finally met the love of my life. And even though I still work hard to find that balance between my desire to be in this relationship and my desire to be alone, I can genuinely say the relationship has never been better. If you are in a relationship and want to take it to the next level or if you're still on the quest of finding your soul mate, here's what I recommend.

• Begin by creating a vision of what your ideal relationship should look like. Identify the qualities you want your soul mate to have. Ask yourself: What would feel so good to me? What do I need? Someone who is kind, spiritually connected, supportive, reliable and generous? Does he or she also want children? The more clarity you have on what qualities you desire, the easier it becomes to attract them into your life.

• Once you have clarity, you must embody those same qualities. And with that embodiment (where you are doing the inner work to become the ideal soul mate for them), you also learn to surrender, trust in the process of life and build the right expectation that as you continue to become this new you, they are moving closer toward you.

• Listen to your intuition as you go about your daily life and notice what you intuitively feel as you interact with new people. If you meet someone, do you feel a sudden wave of chills, a gut feeling of attraction or a flash of insight that you need to speak with this person? Or do you get a stomach cramp, feel sick or distrustful? These are all signals that are meant to keep you on the path of manifesting your ideal relationship.

• Train yourself to let go of shame. This is something many empaths have to continually work on although, to be honest, I think shame is something everyone in society has to deal with. We struggle with sexuality and intimacy when we fail to view our entire bodies as luminous and lovemaking as something sacred. The words Vagina, Penis, and sex evoke a sense of embarrassment and shame for a lot of people. I want to encourage you to see your body with enlightened eyes. Respect your particular aesthetic sensibilities and examine the ones that bring out the feeling of shame in you. Work on this in preparation for your new relationship so that as you manifest your new romance, you can be in a position to awaken sexually and use your intuition to deepen your sexual connection.

Toxic relationships and energy vampires

Sometimes you'll find yourself in a group or engaged in a conversation that almost makes you ill. These types of human interactions often drain your energy; leave you feeling low, offended, unworthy and at times even fearful. It's imperative you recognize the people in your life who uplift you and those that bring you down. Being a sponge to all that's happening around you means you cannot afford to hang out with toxic people or people who love taking advantage of you. Unfortunately, this can be a family member, client, teacher, neighbor, colleague, boss, childhood friend, lover or a strange that sat next to you on the plane. The common name given to such toxic people is "energy vampire" because they seem to suck the life out of you. There are various types of energy vampires. The jealous bees who struggle to feel happy for anyone else, the insecure ones that like to put you and others down to their level of low self-esteem. You know what I mean? They are almost like bullies. Then there are the whiners, the gossipers, the drama queens and so on. I could probably fill up this entire page with this list, but you get the point. The fact of the matter is these types of people are always looking to latch on and feed off others because they have no life force of their own to sustain them. No doubt you've met this group especially because they tend to gravitate toward disempowered empaths because they can sense they will be heard. Now, I'm not here to judge or make anyone wrong, but I do know that you need to steer clear of these people if you want to thrive.

As we get more and more exposed to such people, we soak in that same frequency, and those negative emotions create lots of turbulence within. Dr. Judith Orloff wrote in her book that energy vampires do more than drain your physical energy. The super-malignant ones can make you believe you're an unworthy, unlovable wretch who doesn't deserve any better. She also shares some signs that we need to look out for in her Emotional Freedom book.

Your eyelids get heavy as though you're ready for a nap.
Your mood takes a nosedive.
You want to binge on carbs and other comfort foods.
You feel anxious, depressed or negative even though you don't know why.
You feel put down, sniped at or slimed. Whenever you start to notice any of these changes taking place within you, there's probably an energy vampire around you looking to destabilize your emotional center.

About a year ago one of my close friends started dating a man that seemed very charming. She was definitely smitten and couldn't stop talking about him when they first met. A few weeks into it she started complaining that every time she spends a weekend at his place she usually comes back home feeling more tired than usual. I recommended she paid more attention to what was happening in her body while they were spending time together. That's when she started being mindful of what was happening inside her. After a week of continued self-observation, she realized each time they would meet to go out, she would come back home with a migraine. She assumed it must be her old migraine trying to creep back into her life, but I insisted she takes the time to investigate if there was a connection between her discomforts and this new relationship.

Underneath all the attraction and charm she was experiencing, this guy was certainly not good for her overall wellbeing. It took a while for her to realize he was actually a strong narcissist because somehow she would mute out her intuition whenever he was around but then suffer the consequences later. It was as if she was under a spell. The relationship only lasted a few months because as much as she loved having fun and being reckless with him, she was really struggling with her health and inner peace. Sometimes we find ourselves caught up in this complex situation where the person we care about is just no good for us. The best outcome for everyone concerned is always to walk away.

Protecting yourself from toxic relationships.

It's only natural that I share some prescriptions that can help empower you as you go through your day because we all know there will always be those that we cannot avoid interacting with who aren't good for our well being. Besides, as we move about in society, it's important to make sure we are able to keep off the energetic frequencies that do not serve us and attract more of those that do. Here are some ways you can do that.

• Ground yourself several times throughout the day.

This is best done barefoot and can be as long or as short as you like. You might choose to ground yourself in the morning before engaging with anyone and then do quick short ones throughout the day. The purpose of this technique is to bring yourself back into the present moment, step into your full power and then deal with other people from a position of strength.

Here's how to do it if faced with a stressful situation: Focus on your senses and become aware of your surroundings. Shift your focus from the stressful person and transfer your attention to any soothing sound that you hear blocking out everything else.

• Practice deep breathing before beginning an interaction with someone. Breath control is a highly effective method to bring yourself back into a point of power and can be done instantly. Simply breathe in deeply at intervals for a few minutes until you notice a calming presence taking over your mind and emotions. The more you practice this as you interact with people, the better you'll get at stabilizing your emotions in real time whenever you need it.

- Learn to recognize the type of energy vampire you're having to deal with and protect yourself accordingly.

If for example, you find yourself in the company of a narcissist, realize this person is emotionally limited. Don't make yourself prey to their opinions by attaching your identity or self-worth to them. If interacting with such a person is unavoidable then do your best to communicate with them in a manner that resonates with them and helps them see what's in it for them.

On the other hand, if you're dealing with a borderline personality, the best thing you can do is to stay calm. Practice self-control and avoid reacting just because they push your buttons. Knowing that these types of people feed off anger and enjoy pitting people against each other step away before they include you in rants and anger fest. Refuse to take sides, set clear structures, be firm and let them know your boundaries.

- Find your inner harmony.

Instead of allowing the environment to affect your mood, train your mind and body to find the source of stability within yourself.

- Shield yourself by imagining some shape around your body and aura that keeps you safe from outside energies.

This shield is made of white light that's meant to protect you from any negativity. Now, I will tell you that this is one of the most recommended tactics by many teachers of this topic; however, I don't think it's the best solution. By locking yourself inside your bubble of light, nothing comes in, but nothing flows either. And as you protect yourself from energies, even good energy doesn't come in. In other words, I see it as building up a big wall; sure it keeps the bad guys out, but it also keeps out the good ones.

This might be a great technique to apply when you're just starting out and working on self-mastery but as you learn to handle your sensitivities I encourage you to find techniques that resonate with you which also promote the flow of good energy.

- Find time to be in nature.

For most empaths, nature is the best healer. Whether that's walking on the grass barefoot, on a sandy beach, hugging a tree or whatever else resonates with you. Do this regularly and especially after being exposed to energy vampires so that you can replenish and cleanse your energy.

Parenting

Empathic parents often think there's something wrong with them especially if they don't know of their unique gifts. Relationships, in general, are a challenge, but when you become a parent, it takes things to a whole new level. If you are a parent, this section here is going to help you and those you're raising. But if you're not yet playing the parental role, I suggest skipping over to the next chapter because we are about to jump into the deep end of the struggles that come with being an empath and a parent.

Others might think your overreact or struggle from anxiety problems because of how overwhelmed and burned out you are. While other parents are chilled and barely give their kids a second glance when out and about, you probably spend every minute tracking their every move. You're so attuned to your child that even the slightest change in their mood immediately affects you. When your child falls, you cringe. If she hurts herself or comes home after a bad day at school, you can literally feel her pain. When she has a stomach upset or catches the flu the experience is often more unbearable to you than it is to her. This is a common experience for every empathic parent I know so don't worry, you are not alone, and there's nothing wrong with you.

A recent study showed that children of highly empathic parents thrive and are psychologically and physically healthier, happier and more balanced. I can easily see why that is. Empathic parents create an atmosphere of love, giving, compassion, safety, peace and they are so attuned to their children it's only natural a child will grow up well nurtured. On the other hand, the same study revealed that empathic parents (as great as they are) need to be on the lookout for stress-related problems. Empathic parents tend to have higher inflammation levels because they are always concerned and hyper-vigilant. Being overly cautious and alert is very taxing to your body which as we know becomes detrimental long-term. Being a caring nurturing and thoughtful parent is great, but you must pay attention to your tendencies of going overboard and putting the best interests of others before your own. Yes, I know this is your child, but even so, you still need to tend to your individual needs first unless you want to end up burned out and chronically fatigued.

I want to encourage you to find harmony and create a system of nurturing that works for you and your child. To do this, there are a few practical things you can begin doing today.

- Cultivate emotional resilience.

Learn to detach from what your child is feeling so that you don't feel it so intensely. And yes, there's nothing wrong with detaching from your child's intense emotions from time to time because it helps calm your mind and give you the right perspective. Train your emotions to be less reactive whenever something happens to your child.

- Be more kind to yourself.

Seek to completely eradicate self-criticism, comparing yourself with other parents or judging how you react to situations. Use a kind tone and speak kindly to yourself whenever you carry out an inner dialogue.

- Prioritize some alone time regularly so you can refuel.

All empaths need time alone to unwind and rejuvenate, but I know things get tough once you become a parent. The only time you have alone might be during bathroom breaks, and you know what, if that's all you can get, then make the most of it. Schedule a specific time of the day where your "bathroom break" is actually an alone time where you can just be with yourself. Of course, if you can engage in some activity that helps you refuel like taking a long salt bath, walking in nature, reading a book, praying or whatever gets you in the zone, then, by all means, do it regularly.

- Learn to create distance whenever you feel emotional imbalance creeping in.

Unless you want to constantly spiral into anxiety or get stuck in a foul mood that seems to come from nowhere, I recommend you get into the habit of taking a step back and allowing your emotions to process when you get triggered. Analyze your emotions, find the source of negativity and release them.

• Set clear boundaries for everyone in the family including your child.
You need to teach your child what healthy boundaries in your family set-up look like. This isn't going to be easy because sooner or later your child will realize other kids have it differently and it may raise some comparison issues. This is where you'll have to be firm, loving and creative with how things run in your home. Find a middle ground that works for both you and the child especially if they are old enough to carry personal preferences as well.

• Ban any and all emotional drama.
Empaths cannot handle emotional tension, yelling, and conflict very well. We also cannot thrive around negativity. As such, it is imperative that you teach your child the difference between negative and positive emotions as early on as possible. Help them understand the importance of communicating honestly, peacefully and thoughtfully. Show them how to practice self-control and how to avoid the common trap of emotional selfishness.

• Take it one day at a time.
Being a parent is a hard job for anyone. Add in our empathic sensitivities and tendencies to seek solitude, and the challenge quadruples. You will be challenged a lot but the reward will be even greater, and the stronger your connection and understanding with your child, the more enjoyable the journey will be.

The more you can take care of yourself and build up your emotional resilience the more you will have to give to your family. Now, what if you're raising an empathic child?

Raising empathic children

In our highly insensitive society, it's your job as a parent to recognize if your child is an empath. Empathic children have nervous systems that rapidly react to strong external stimuli including stress. They feel too much and frequently don't know how to manage this sensory overload. The main problem is that the children can't yet articulate what they are experiencing. This was one of the main issues I faced growing up. I realized that I see more, hear more, smell more and experience more emotions than the other kids around me. I was highly intuitive at a very young age and could tell when my parents were fighting even if I didn't hear them doing it. I could tell when something was wrong with my teacher even when she was trying hard to act normal in class. Strong smells, bright lights, and loud talking really affected me, and I preferred to be on my own or with a few close friends. Most people in school called me shy, weak and antisocial.

In fact, I can recall one time in 4th grade during playtime we had a substitute teacher who found it very odd that I was sitting in class blissfully coloring my favorite mandala. He called me over and asked me if there was something wrong with me. "No," I responded with a smile. He wanted to know if the other kids were refusing to play with me or if I was hurt by something. When I told him I was just enjoying my coloring session, he looked puzzled. So just to ease his discomfort, I decided to spend a few minutes outside playing with the other kids. It's tough to be an empathic child in a world that misjudges your behavior and tries to force you to fit in with the other kids. But empathic children can never fit in and when we force them to do things they aren't comfortable with we trigger unnecessary stress and negative emotional experiences.

As a parent, you need to discern as early on as possible whether you have an empathic child or not because as I said, they won't be able to tell you. Some signs to look out for include:
Your child gets overwhelmed really quickly. Both stimuli and school always overwhelm him or her. If you're out in a mall or a big party, your child will choose to cling on to you and stay by your side. You'll notice they are experiencing every smell, all the loud voices, and sounds around them. When the teacher yells or gives too much homework, they will come home completely distraught and feeling defeated.

Try this:
Get to know the triggers that destabilize your child and help to reduce them as much as possible. Have a word with the teachers if you need to and perhaps don't take them into the mall when it's busiest.

- You'll notice your child cries when others around them are hurt or upset. If you see an ad on TV showing how children are dying from lack of water and food and your child immediately falls apart, he or she is probably an empath. You might also have noticed they get sobby whenever there's a family feud at home or if one of their friends gets mad, hurt or upset.

Try this:

Teach your child to be grounded and to center their own energy whenever they experience that discomfort from others. Help them distinguish when they are mirroring other people's emotions and show them how to stay in the present moment. Once your child learns to be calm in an uncomfortable situation praise them for being kind and concerned for others and then offer a way of helping out that helps them detach. This will look different for every situation but let me share an example of something my mom taught me.

I remember a time when my best friend came to school with swollen eyes. She had been crying all night and all morning. Her parents were getting divorced, and she would be staying with her mom while her dad was moving to another state. It was tragic. Seeing her that way immediately made me sick. That day I couldn't even have lunch. We just sat next to each other in the school cafeteria in silence and barely touched our food. By the time I got home that evening I had a terrible headache, my tummy was all knotted up, and I had this heaviness in my chest that made it hard to breathe. At first, my mom thought I was catching something. She checked my fever and was about to suggest we pay the doctor's office a visit when she paused, took a deep breath in and asked me if anything strange had happened at school. I shared the whole story (in sobs) after which we just sat there in silence with her arms around me.

After what seemed like a really long time for me, she asked me if I wanted to try something that would help me feel better and also help my friend. We sat down on the carpet, clasped hands and she took me through some kind of a breathing technique. Initially, I didn't want to do it, but seeing her do it and knowing that it might help my friend somehow, I stuck with it. A few minutes later I felt very calm, and the heaviness in my chest was gone. Then she asked me, " are you feeling hurt right now?"

"I don't know," I said. She told me she was very proud of how much I care about the people around me and especially my friend. Then she explained that adults behave in strange ways sometimes and can hurt us without meaning to but, if I want to be an excellent friend I need to be strong and loving and reliable and encouraging so that my friend can find a way through this challenging phase. It totally resonated with me. The more I become a loving friend, the more she would stop feeling like all was lost. So my mom asked me if there was anything special I wanted to do for my friend to remind her of how much I love her. I immediately jumped up in excitement. "Yes. I want to bake her favorite cookies and take them to school tomorrow", I said. Mom was more than happy to help me bake and delighted me, even more, when she said that we could take them to her house before dinner time that same day. I can't tell you what a difference that single experience made in my life and I have carried on that ritual of approaching pain and hurt the same way.

Your child is unique and may require a different approach, it's up to you to find what works for you. No one in my life understood me for a big part of my life, but my mother always did. Even though she's not an empath and had no knowledge of what empaths are, she did see me as a sensitive child and did an excellent job helping me manage my sensitivities while growing up. Dr. Judith Orloff has an assessment that can help you score your child's level of sensitivity. Answer the questions below, and if you get 9-12 yesses, then your child is an extreme empath. If you get 6-9 yesses, then your child is a strong empath. 4-8 yesses indicate your child is moderate and 1-3 indicates your child possess some empathic traits.

1. Does he or she feel things deeply?
2. Does he or she get over-stimulated by people, large crowds, noise or stress?
3. Does he or she have strong reactions to sad or frightening scenes in books or movies?
4. Does he or she want to escape and hide from family gatherings because there's too much going on?
5. Does he or she feel "different" than the other kids or complain about not fitting in?
6. Is he or she a good listener and compassionate with others?
7. Does he or she have a strong connection to nature, animals, plants or stuffed animals?
8. Does he or she require a lot of time alone rather than playing with other kids?
9. Does he or she take on your own or other people's emotions or stress - and act out when you're angry upset or depressed?
10. Does he or she have one best friend and a few good friends rather than a vast social network?

Here are a few tips to help you create more of that calm, nurturing, and safe environment for your empathic child so both of you can enjoy this ride even more.

• Be an emotional coach.
Your child doesn't have the emotional vocabulary needed to communicate what they are experiencing effectively. It is your job to help them learn how to name and tame the emotions that show up. Talk openly about feelings and guide them to become emotionally literate. Find moments daily where you connect face-to-face and listen to them. Validate your child's feelings by acknowledging what you're picking up from them. When they seem sad, let them know "you seem sad, is everything okay?" Point out feelings in books, films that you watch together or people that you encounter. Use stories and emotional words to teach them things.

• Increase their self-awareness.
Make your child aware of their unique ability to feel, sense and experience everything deeply. Help him, or her discern the difference between emotions that stream out of their own consciousness and those that they pick up from other people including you. The more aware they can become, the easier it will be to gain emotional mastery and become warrior empaths as they grow.

• Create rituals for grounding.
This is one of the main things I would love every empathic child to learn even before they can write. It helps alleviate so much of the stress and suffering that they would be exposed to as they grow. I wish I had learned how to ground and center myself as a child. But hey, at least you can pass it down to your child and save them a lot of pain and heartache. The younger the child, the more you'll need to improvise but if the child is old enough, teach them the grounding method in this book as well as some of the practices I will be sharing on the chapter on self-care.

• Set a regular "decompress" time.
Your child needs time to unwind and refuel himself or herself. Make sure they have time daily to do this especially if they are already going to school and interacting with the society a lot.

• Teach them how to focus on the process and growth, not the goals.

I know it will be tempting to get your child into goal setting, beating everyone in the class and completing tasks so that teachers and others feel good. Instead, I want to encourage you to train your child to stay on his or her own path or growth and learning. Empaths will always do things differently, and it's crucial as children they learn that the process is just as important as the achievement.

• Create an emotional container that supports your child and helps them feel safe, heard and loved.

Let your child know that they can count on you no matter what. As you do, your child will start to develop strong self-regulation skills. They will also have the courage to process emotions and be proud of their sensitivities and unique abilities. As we all know, that sense of empowerment leads to very active, happy and prosperous members of society. One cannot give what one doesn't have. Empathic children can only grow up to be influential leaders in our community if we do a good job creating a space for them where they feel good about who they are. An environment that creates security and emotional stability so that they don't have to go through life on defense mode, fighting against an invisible enemy.

• Allow your child to see your vulnerability.

This is not something you'll hear mainstream parents talking about. Most parents believe in masking their emotions in front of their children. Not that it works, but at least some manage to get away with it for a while. As a parent raising an empath, however, you don't stand a chance at success if you try to pull this off. Your child will always know what's happening with you whether you admit it or not. Instead of creating a relationship with him or her that's based on lying, why not share the journey together. It's okay for your child to see you stumble and fall in your dreams, your emotional mastery, and growth as a human being. The more you can show your child that life is about progress, not perfection and that there is strength in vulnerability, the stronger he or she will be too. Sounds counterintuitive I know, but just test it for a while. It will strengthen your relationship and take off unnecessary pressure for you and your child.

The fact that both of you have come to enjoy this human journey as companions as miraculous and perfect enough. There's no need to "pretend" or "fake it." As I said, it's about focusing on the process and the progress, not the goals. If you genuinely believe that, then it's time you emulate it in your life. Being vulnerable doesn't have to be something extraordinary. Something as simple as apologizing to your child when you've made a mistake or sharing a lesson you've learned from interacting with someone can help develop a sense of stability and normalcy with your child.

Chapter 04: Work and Career

Job satisfaction seems to be elusive for most people on the planet. In the United States of America alone, at least fifty percent of workers report being unsatisfied and unhappy with their jobs. That's literally half the workforce. For empaths and highly sensitive individuals, that dissatisfaction runs deeper than just a paycheck and healthcare insurance. The daily challenges involved in working a regular job creates more stress than is necessary plunging most empaths deeper into that pit of despair we all need to avoid. You'll be hard pressed to go online and find anything remotely empowering about being an empath and thriving at work. Much of what you'll find are people sharing this perception that being an empath is difficult, and work is a constant struggle.

People want to take advantage of you, they might bully you, and no one ever recognizes all your dedication. We are warned that we have to be extra careful because energy vampires and narcissists at work are out to get us and prey on our abilities. Most people seem to be taking such a disempowering stand. But does it really help?

I'm not here to argue with any of these suggestions, and you know, maybe some of this information is true, but you need to be aware of the fact that your mindset and how you approach your work is what determines your experience. It is true that as an empath you will have to process and manage the energies of everyone else you work with. And that the sounds, scents, and details that most people hardly ever notice will be at the foreground for you, but that doesn't mean work should be an ongoing punishment. I want to invite you to step into a more empowering state and tell a new story about your work experience. There is a new way to be an empath and having gone through ways you can thrive in your relationships, it's time to shift focus and talk about how you can do the same when it comes to your career and business.

Being an empath is a big gift that comes with great power. With that power comes even greater responsibility and the more you learn to develop yourself the more you'll become an empowered empath. What many of us don't realize is that there are two types of empaths roaming around this planet teaching on this topic. The empowered empath who has developed himself/herself and teaches from a place of strength and self-mastery. Then there's the disempowered empath. He or she teaches from a place of victimhood and lacks the self-mastery and mental strength needed to handle his or her sensitivities. In other words, an underdeveloped empath. Depending on whose material you come across, you'll be on the receiving end of disempowering information that keeps you walking the path of struggle in your work, relationships, health, and personal fulfillment or empowering information so you can start walking the path of prosperity. I am taking a stand on being an empowered empath even at work because I know how possible it can be for all of us to thrive. I hope this book is helping you come to the same realization.

The fact that you can detect and process energy better than most people around you means that you have the power of understanding and handling work relationships better than the average person (assuming you've developed yourself). Many empaths struggle to find a job that is the right fit because they are looking for happiness in all the wrong places. As such every day feels exhausting. It is true there are overly stressful jobs that are perhaps not ideal for empaths and highly sensitive people. The amount of stimulation in such a work environment can cause a great deal of stress, overwhelm and frustration making it less ideal for the average empath but I can assure, in any "high pressure" job you could think of, I bet there exists an empath who is thriving. For example, I've met doctors, lawyers and even got to interview a military guy who is an empath. This leads me to believe that as long as you find a job that is the right fit for your unique talents and continue to develop yourself, there's no limit to where you could work. But above all else, if you want to find a job that satisfies you, the first step is to step out of a victim mindset.

Michelle, a client of mine, shared with me how unbearable life was becoming for her. We bumped into each other through a synchronistic experience when we sat together during a flight and immediately shared a connection. At the time she felt tired of the boss that was bullying her and the narcissistic colleagues that she believed were trying to manipulate and control her. The ongoing story in her mind was that she was being treated with so much hostility and that her overdue promotion had been overlooked because she's not as outspoken as the rest of the loud-mouthed personalities working with her. I pointed out that her only chance at having the life and career she wanted was to take full responsibility for her own power. She needed to stop victimizing herself and positioning her boss as the big bad wolf in her story. The reason I insisted on this is that I know nothing good can come from playing the victim. One might look for a new job, a new partner or new friends but if there's no change in mindset, even the new manifestations will turn out just as ugly.

All this is to remind you that as I share tips on how you can thrive and manifest your dream role it's important to realize that you are the determining factor. Your success and happiness at work depend primarily on your mindset, and that's where you should start making changes if you want something new. In addition to working on your mindset and choosing to become an empowered empath, I also want you to consider choosing work that aligns with your values and supports your talents. This will make the work experience way more enjoyable. Most people are choosing jobs because of pay or because "nothing else is available," which is such a disservice to their own well-being. We live in a digital age where you can be anything and work from anywhere. Whether it's a job or a business, go for something that compliments who you are as an individual. Consider the company culture you're getting into and the skills you'll need to excel and thrive in that role. I understand that we all have bills to pay, but surely you know of people who have found a way to pay bills and do work that fulfills them. Why shouldn't you have the same opportunity as well?

Recommended Jobs For Empaths.

I think any job or business can help you create your dream lifestyle as long as you've done the research. As I mentioned, even doctors can be empaths, so it isn't so much about limiting yourself to focus on a particular career. It's more about finding the right fit. And since empaths are unique individuals, there cannot be a one size fits all. Therefore, you might not resonate with any of the job suggestions I offer here, and that's okay. Use these as inspiration to help you tap into what lights you up. Experts studying and working with empaths and highly sensitive individuals put this list together. Based on their research, these jobs stand to create an environment that an empath would most likely enjoy.

- Fashion Designer.
- Interior Designer.
- Graphics Designer.
- Analyst.
- IT professional.

- Accountant.
- Animal Rescue.
- Musician.
- Actor.
- Massage therapist.
- Life coach.
- Writer.
- Artist.
- Counselor.
- Music teacher.
- Business Owner.
- Caregiver.
- Botanist.

How to manifest your dream career as an empath.

What many companies are beginning to realize is that empaths have a lot of strengths that positively impact a company's overall performance. Our ability to pay close attention, genuinely listen and understand the needs of others is integral to building a strong team. It's also a great superpower to have when serving a customer. That's why this is the best time for empaths to step up and step out boldly into the marketplace. You need to sharpen your skills, get clear on the role you want to play and reach for your dream job because I can assure you, the business world is ready to embrace leaders like you and me. If you want to build your career working for a company or on your own, here are some ideas to help you land your dream role.

- Start with your "Why."

Simon Sinek says, "people don't buy WHAT you do; they buy WHY you do it." Instead of focusing solely on what you want, I suggest you take time to figure out why you want it. Take some quiet time and journal the answer to this question: Why do you want this dream career?

I know you already have the details of your dream job outlined. But that won't be enough to help you land it. You also need clarity on why you want it so that you can clearly detect if the job interview or business niche you want to step into aligns with your values and beliefs.

• Get to know your talents and unique gifts.

Before others can learn to appreciate and value your work, they must see what you bring to the table. That implies you need to know your talents well enough to put them on the table in a way that brings value to the other person. Knowing your sensitivities, strengths, and abilities help you demonstrate to another person effortlessly. Answer these questions: What are your unique talents? What are your sensitivities? How do you see this benefiting a fellow human being?

• Understand your temperament.

If you don't know yourself and the triggers that take you off balance, it'll be hard to spot the best opportunity to cease. You need to understand the environments that help you thrive and increase your productivity so that as you go for an interview, you'll be testing to see if the working conditions will help you produce your best stuff or not. What circumstances do you feel enable you to do your best work? For example, do you enjoy working alone? In absolute silence? With music in the background? Do you feel good working with a team?

• Get your story right.

Take stock of your past experience, skills you have, all your sensitivities and gifts. Then use all these positives to direct your next career role. If you realize like the dog-walking girl, I spoke about earlier in the book that you are an animal empath and communicate naturally with all kinds of animals, use that to your advantage. It could mean you need to develop additional skills and get training to get into the medical field if that's the direction you want to go, or like her, it could be that you just need to grow a client base that trusts you. Then from there, you can start offering higher services that produce a good income. Everything depends on the story you tell yourself and how developed your talents are. Before you go hunting for your next job, do this part diligently.

• Quit idealizing this concept of "dream job for an empath."
It only leads to procrastination and unnecessary disappointment. Instead of holding this perception, focus on consciously building a lifestyle and work role that you love. Something that you do which feels meaningful to you where you make a difference in the lives of others. Create a vision for yourself and then live from that desired state. I say this because I think for many of us, this idea of a dream career or business is actually centered on a feeling of fear and lack. As strange as it may sound, most of us are trying to remedy this feeling of being different from everyone else by creating this idea that there has to be a "special" type of job for people like us. But if you think about it, people like us are here to help heal, spread light, love, and compassion in the world. I believe every industry and niche market needs that. I would rather have a doctor who is an empath treating me instead of a non-empath. I'd rather have a hairdresser who is an empath doing my hair, and I'd undoubtedly choose an accountant who is an empath to help me understand taxes. Wouldn't you?

The key to creating a world where empaths are leaders and non-empaths learn to practice a little more compassion is to change how we perceive ourselves. We need to view our work as a way of fulfilling a specific purpose in our lives. It's an invitation to turn a new leaf and to get more real with yourself.

What would you love to contribute to this world?

Before you go out and take on interviews or start that business venture, make these adjustments. Then discipline yourself to carry out the new changes, and before long, new opportunities to serve fellow human beings will present themselves.

Tips To Empower Yourself At Work

• Define what happiness and success feel and look like for you.
No two people (even empaths) share the same definition when it comes to success and happiness. That means you need to redefine what a successful career or job ought to feel and look like. Make sure you know your values and goals and check to see they align with your work.

- Choose career objectives that bring you the highest satisfaction, not others.

Put your needs first and choose to focus on the goals and objectives that bring out the best in you. Goals that make you come alive and feel a sense of fulfillment as you move toward them. As an empowered empath, you have given up the need to do what others expect. You recognize that tending to your needs actually makes you better and creates that energy that's needed to support others without sacrificing yourself.

- Seek a mentor or community that gets you.

Having a guide as you progress in your career whether you choose to be employed or self-employed is vital to your success. That's why every successful individual in the world has at least one mentor. The good news is that you can have a mentor who is also an empath or a highly sensitive person. Someone who is empowered and demonstrates how to live the kind of life you aspire to have. In today's world (thanks to technology) this is easy to arrange. But even if for whatever reason getting a guide isn't possible you can always find a supportive community of like-minded people.

- Don't take things personally.

Most people are usually projecting their unresolved issues and insecurities when they interact with you. Learn to be more light-hearted with other people's comments and opinion.

- Align with your soul and listen to your intuition more before taking action.

Since you play the game of energy, it is crucial to align yourself fully and bring in that higher aspect of you into your daily activities. This will enable you to receive more intuitive guidance and make your actions more productive.

- Set clear energetic boundaries.

Even if you work in an open space in a chaotic office, you can create a sacred "zone" for yourself around your desk with the energetic frequency you want to be in. Using plants, pictures of loved ones or pets or other creative fun ways can create a psychological barrier.

- Create the right atmosphere for yourself.

Do you prefer silence or some background music? Learn to recognize the sights, sounds, smells and other elements that foster a calm, productive state. Find ways to incorporate these things into your workspace whether you work in an office or at home.

- Take frequent breaks to recharge.

It's essential to take short walks, bathroom breaks, water breaks and even short meditative breaks throughout the workday. Many offices today are also creating a uniquely quiet space where one can refuel during the day. If you work from home, then make sure you create a space that enables you to this or schedule short walks around the block.

- Focus on and gravitate toward coworkers that inspire and energize you. Invest your free time on people who uplift you, make you laugh and support your creativity so your time can be more taken up by inspiration. This will help fuel your mood, problem-solving skills, and productivity.

- Choose to make your work about creating meaning and serving others. This is a mindset shift that only you can make. If you decide that your work can and will make a difference in the world, then everything you do will be influenced by that attitude of mind. Don't be reactive; be proactive in all that you do. Your work might be demanding with crazy deadlines but only you can reframe it into something empowering that makes you feel like you're contributing positively.

Chapter 05: Empaths and Self Care

Self-care is crucial to thriving for empaths and highly sensitive people. That includes taking care of yourself both inside and out. In this chapter, we are devoting all our attention to the practices that will help us nurture ourselves first. As all empaths know, putting our needs first is usually quite challenging. As empaths, we naturally extend love outwards and shower others with boundless compassion, affection, and generosity. But have you noticed how hard it can be to point that same level of affection and attention inward?

The very gift that makes us highly attuned to others and their energy combined with our natural tendency to be over giving can spiral into negativity if we neglect our needs. You may not fully believe that you deserve to give yourself the same gifts you often give to others (even those who don't deserve it), but I assure you, no one is more deserving. And you probably need it more than anyone else given all the hardships you've had to endure. Giving is only good to you and the receiver when you give from a place of abundance and overflow. Yet many empaths ignore this natural law of success. In fact, most of us fall into depression, anxiety and we suffer from things like insomnia precisely because we forget to point our gifts inward.

Let's touch on that a bit more here.

Adrenal Fatigue, Exhaustion, and Insomnia. Breaking free of the zombie life.

Adrenal fatigue is a condition many empaths will be familiar with. It is a collection of symptoms such as anxiety, insomnia, body aches, trouble thinking clearly, anxiety and exhaustion. The theory around this condition is that the adrenal glands and hormones such as cortisol that keep you energized start getting depleted because they are unable to deal with the external stress you are exposed to. Given the sensitive nature of empaths, when one hasn't yet developed into an empowered empath, it's easy to see how the daily sensory overload and stressful conditions can quickly lead to such an illness. Unfortunately, toxic people, toxic environments and feeling powerless can lead to endless pain issues and diseases.

Have you ever tossed and turned in bed for hours because you just couldn't fall asleep because of how hyperactive your mind was? Your body might be tired, but if your mind and emotions don't calm down, getting peaceful rest is dreadful. What's worse is that after a while you begin to experience emotional and physical fatigue because you're not recharging.

At the beginning of this book, I shared with you the story of how awful things used to be in my world. I would wake up sick and tired, literally. My body ached, I was exhausted and stressed and felt like a needed a reset button. But there was none. My body was under so much stress, and my adrenal glands were terribly over stimulated so I would go from having lots of energy and not being able to sleep for a few weeks then take a dip to the other side where I felt like I had no energy to get up and shower.

At first, I tried to remedy the lack of energy with coffee and sugar, which was a huge mistake. In the end, I had to get some professional help because I finally broke into full-blown insomnia and adrenal fatigue.

It's not easy taking full responsibility for your own emotions and still being able to handle all the energy around you. Especially in our current society. As our minds try to figure out what's happening to combat the discomfort we experience, we must do our part to increase self-awareness so we can recognize what's happening. So in all this discomfort, what should you do?

- Regularly get your cortisol levels measured. Keep a close eye on that and if you're really not in a good place, have your physician prescribe a natural cortisol replacement to help you get back in shape.
- Rest as much as you can. Please sleep for more hours. I cannot emphasize this enough. When I was struggling the most, I was also sleeping the least. There is a direct correlation between how much good sleep you get and how good you feel.
- Learn to manage incoming energy in better more empowering ways. As often as possible "return to sender" the energy that you've picked up which doesn't serve you.
- Create bedtime rituals that take you to a happy place and foster harmony.
- Stay away from stimulants like coffee. If you must have it, don't do it close to your bedtime.

• Work on your mindset and choose to empower yourself so that you can be more in charge and in control of how you feel.

These are just a few things you can already start doing today to help eliminate the struggle that so many of us face. Walking around like a zombie is no fun and messes with your productivity and progress in life.

To counter all the negativity that usually proceeds when an empath neglects his or her own needs, I will be sharing a long list of practices you can start implementing into your daily routine. Pick and choose a handful and test them out to see which resonate with you the most. Not all these practices will suit you so don't feel pressure to use something just because you were told it works. We are all unique and what works for me may not yield highly positive results for another.

If you are a parent raising an empathic or highly sensitive child, these tips are a great way to help them handle their sensitivities better, but you may want to tweak them a bit depending on your particular situation and the age of your child.

One more thing before we start getting into practices. Don't do this from a place of obligation or because your guru says you must. If you're not yet sold on the importance of prioritizing self-care then educate yourself some more on the benefits. Then check in with yourself to see what things feel like currently and compare and contrast the changes that would come about if you were to make the shit.

Importance of Self Care For An Empath And Highly Sensitive People

Self-nurturing, self-compassion, and self-care are integral to the healing of your relationship with yourself. This is what you need if you want to feel whole, fulfilled and secure in this life. Many of us go searching for this feeling in all the wrong places. We seek it in others, in dream jobs, in intimate relationships and so on but the only place we can find it is in the healing of the Self. Learning to love yourself is perhaps one of the biggest jobs you'll ever do because as you start working on yourself, you'll realize there are a lot of self-worth issues to overcome.

By choosing to tend to your own needs and prioritize self-care, you'll start feeling more in charge of your own emotions and sensitivities. You'll no longer feel like you're "too fragile" or at the mercy of other people. There will also be a sense of relief as you go about your day and things will start to feel more balanced. It's definitely going to get easier for you to say no when it feels right for you because in essence your intuition will become strengthened. Exerting healthy boundaries (something many of us struggle with) for yourself and others will feel less awkward, and no one will shame or guilt you into taking time for yourself. I also discovered in my own journey that I had more clarity, an increased mental focus, more energy and I felt more inspired to work on the projects that matter to me. Self-care isn't just about taking care of your physical needs although it does include that. Real self-care includes nourishing your mind, body, and spirit.

Physical self-care is a common one. It involves taking care of your body internally and externally. This includes eating the right food, self-grooming, engaging in some form of physical activity regularly, getting enough sleep and staying hydrated.

Mental self-care is just as important as physical self-care and involved giving your mind just the right amount of stimulation to keep it sharp, active and focused. This can be done through reading, engaging in deep conversation with someone you strongly connect with or even listening to inspiring podcasts and learning something new.

Emotional self-care gives us the mastery we need to step out of survival mode and into thriving mode as empaths. Because we detect and process energy at heightened levels, emotional self-care is something we cannot afford to skip over. Our emotional well-being and overall health depend on it because what we hold on the inside materializes on the outside as our reality. That's why we must engage daily in some form of emotional processing and release of feelings that are active within us. We can do it with a trusted friend, journal it down, or speak to a therapist. We can also choose fun ways to help us dissolve and release negative emotions through composing music, listening to music, dancing, drawing, poetry singing, etc.

Spiritual self-care is something no one can ever tell you how to do it right. It is such a personal and intimate experience that only you can discover through your own sacred experiments. Spiritual self-care means different things to different people and usually comes down to the ideologies you hold. Maybe you associate it with cultural tradition, or perhaps for you, it's religious. Regardless of your concept, what matters is that you are nurturing yourself spiritually. It's one of the most important aspects of self-care especially if you are looking to eradicate that feeling of loneliness, "not belonging," feeling unloved and alone. A permanent and real sense of oneness, belonging, connectedness and self-acceptance take place when you feed yourself spiritually either through reading spiritual books, Yoga, Meditation, spending time in nature and other spiritual practices. In the last chapter, we dive more into spiritual awakening and what that means for an empath so if you've been curious about this topic keep turning the pages.

Life-supporting activities also require some conscious self-care because these are the practical things that make your life more comfortable. Things like housework chores, grocery shopping, finances, and logistics are all tasks that can at times feel burdensome, and that drains our energy. However, we can choose to practice a little self-care and self-awareness as we go through these tasks, which helps us feel a sense of accomplishment. For example, I decided I would rearrange the furniture in my home using Feng Shui. I decluttered my closet and set up a little "calm zone" area for myself. I am also getting into the habit of setting up auto-pay on my essential monthly bills so that I don't have to deal with running late on my payments. And I consciously watch my inner dialogue whenever I am paying for things in the supermarket or at a restaurant because I want my money talk to shift from lack to abundance. These little shifts that I am prioritizing are taking mundane everyday chores and turning them into moments where I can deliberately practice self-love.

All this to say that self-care is something that must capture all aspects of your life. Leave no area unattended especially the daily mundane stuff that usually burdens you. Use every opportunity to show yourself how much you care and love yourself. The more you can give to yourself and evoke within you that feeling of being loved and cared for, the easier it will be to give to others from a place of overflow. The trick here is to hold the right energy space for others as you manage and master your own emotions and energy.

Finding Your True Self

Before you can really embrace, accept and love yourself fully you must shift the perception you hold about who you really are. What does it really mean to you to be your true Self?

Do you currently feel like you are being yourself? And do you even like yourself? For many empaths, saying yes requires effort. Too many false conditioning and low self-esteem stand in the way of that positive perception. But here's the thing... To thrive as an empath, you must be yourself. And to be yourself, you've got to know who you are. Your sense of identity and the self-image you hold about yourself will never allow you to step into a state of empowerment unless you build a strong, stable ground from which to stand. For a long time, I used to say, " I just want to be myself but I don't know how." It was the imprisoned aspect of me that was seeking freedom. But freedom from what?

This is a profound question that requires contemplation, reflection, and lifelong exploration because we are all seeking that same freedom. What I'm sure of is that this freedom can only happen when we begin to realize there is a version of us "invisible to the outside world" that holds all the answers. And part of practicing self-care is acknowledging that the more we point self-compassion, forgiveness, self-love, and affection inward, the more we are inviting this other "Self" to flow into our consciousness and actively engage with us. There is great power in this and as any empowered empath will tell you, learning to open up to and connect with that other Self will give your whole life new meaning and shed light on why you are here and why you possess the gifts and sensitivities that make you an empath.

I hope you are starting to see why self-care isn't just something nice to do for yourself; it is the key to the freedom that you seek.

Locating And Healing Your Emotional Triggers

We all have those super-reactive buttons inside of us that become activated by someone else's behavior, comment or energy. It is imperative we become aware of these buttons so we can create a buffer time to help us avoid that natural tendency to become reactive. Our human mind is inherently impatient and has all kinds of hang-ups and emotional reactions especially when our ideas about how things should be collide with how things are. As empaths, we are experts at self-torment and self-manufactured pain whether we realize it or not. Usually, it's because we make choices, say things or hold ourselves back and postpone our happiness because we don't feel deserving enough. It seems we've become so accustomed to "settling" for coping mechanisms and survival guides that no other life seems possible at present. When something is always missing or when we still feel inferior to the present circumstances, it becomes easy to fall for the trap of self-loathing and judgment. This can be a great source of emotional pain. A wound is created, and whenever someone happens to press on that wound, we immediately react. Through the mind, many of us have created a prison of suffering (empaths all believe in the great suffering), and we forget that we are the architects of our lives. You hold the key that can and will set you free.

Read that last statement several times. Breathe it in, contemplate, pray and meditate over it until it feels true for you because in reality, until you start believing that you hold the key to freedom and success, the "great suffering" will continue to consume you. By becoming aware of and uncovering the false perceptions that cause you to cling to pain and suffering you can open up to a deep experience of peace and heal your triggers. For example, if someone tells you that you don't have what it takes to manifest true love in your life because you can only attract narcissists, and you overreact, it indicates there's a trigger there. There must be a place in you that is emotionally wounded by that statement. Is it because that has been your past experience? Is it because that's what you secretly believe as well? Or could it be that you don't feel worthy of love?

When you catch yourself reacting, lashing out, getting defensive, angry or resentful, stop, breathe, distance yourself from that heated moment and address your emotional issues. You might think that the other person is wrong for being so rude and insensitive, but in actuality, if you hadn't allowed other forces and factors to dictate your behavior, you'd have no reason to be affected by this. Being aware of your actions and behavior rather than dwelling on what the other person is doing or saying is where you need to focus your attention. Your emotional triggers are wounds that need to heal. The best way to do this is by practicing self-compassion and mental cleansing. You need to know what beliefs you hold and why you still hold them. Many empaths have grown up in environments that traumatized them emotionally, and so it's only natural that some of those wounds still need healing. For example, children who grew up feeling helpless will probably experience panic and overwhelm whenever they're in a new situation. And if assigned large projects with very little time they might crack under that pressure, not because they're not good enough but because the workload triggers a wound that still needs healing. If someone around makes a comment around their inability to perform the task properly, this triggers an emotional and sometimes physical reaction that can lead to anger, binge eating, over drinking, etc. The best way to free yourself from such experiences now and in the future is by learning to release and heal those wounds. When you find yourself overcome by negative emotions, test out some of these tips to see which ones bring you back to peace and well-being.

Tip One: Resist the natural impulse to judge your feelings as bad and definitely don't ignore them. Every emotion you experience believe it or not can teach you something about yourself. Ask what the emotion is trying to tell you and listen with great intent as your body picks up the message.

Tip Two: Practice self-compassion as soon as you catch yourself falling for the negative energies. Speak words of encouragement and love. You can say, "this too shall pass" or "whatever fear says, I know nothing can destroy me." Cling to the knowing that regardless of what's happening, the real you is strong and bigger than any condition.

Tip Three: Switch your perspective and be more objective about your emotions. As you catch yourself being sucked into a negative spiral, rather than resist (what you resist persists) simply ground yourself and let that energy flow. If you identify with negativity and acknowledge "I am angry" or "I am depressed," it's super hard to detach and let go. That's why you want to train yourself to see emotions as moving energy like electricity. Think of a beautiful chandelier hanging in a hotel lobby. When the lights are switched on, electricity flows and illuminates the chandelier. We can distinguish that moving electricity is not the chandelier. Similarly, your emotions flow through you, but they are not who you really are.

Tip Four: Perhaps this is the first tip I should have started with because it truly is the starting point of any transformation. Take full responsibility over your life and the emotions that dominate your day. If you catch yourself reacting to certain people and situations in the same way, rather than label them bad, ask yourself what you need to learn and do to change that automatic response.

Tip Five: Be willing to heal your emotions. Don't let your ego tell you that there's something wrong with you or worse yet, that there's nothing you can do about how others make you feel. The reactions you experience are only responses and even though you might not always know what to do to heal, simply declaring that you are open, willing and ready to heal allows the process to begin.

Tip Six: Journal about the origin of your triggers as you become aware of them. If like in the example I shared above you realize something happened while you were a child that caused you to feel wounded, now you have the opportunity to rewrite that story with greater awareness. Once you track and find the origin of the emotional wound, I want you to tear off those pages of the old story, burn or shred them into pieces then start again with the new permanent story that you want to attach to that phase of your past.

Tip Seven: Reprogram your false beliefs as you become aware of the triggers. Start with the trigger that has the least emotional charge. Compassionately tell yourself "this is not my reality anymore. What is true is that I am deserving of love, I am intelligent, I am capable of greatness, I am good enough." Whatever wound you still have, find it's ideal opposite and replace the old conviction with this new one.

Tip Eight: If this feels too much for you to bear, consider getting assistance from a trained professional or at the very least, a trusted loved one. Surround yourself with people you love and respect, let them know what you're working on so they can help you during those reactive moments. If you don't want to do this with a family member or friend you could choose to join a group therapy or seek expert help from someone trained in the field of psychiatry or emotional trauma. Just make sure it is someone you naturally vibe with because having that natural chemistry will aid the healing you want to experience.

Nutrition And Exercise

Before you can find peace, freedom, and a sense of fulfillment and thrive in your life, you must find harmony. Moreso, what I am referring to here is inner harmony and what's commonly referred to as homeostasis.

This is a quest many human beings are on whether consciously or unconsciously because whenever the physical body is not in homeostasis, nothing else really works. Do you agree?

Well, for empaths and highly sensitive people the urgency of creating good eating habits is more pronounced. The way I like to say it is that we have a short karmic leash. We can't get away with half of what the average human can do whether that means indulging with negativity, binge-eating or neglecting our bodies. If we don't cleanse our energy and generate productive emotions, we suffer more than the average person. Similarly, if we don't eat right, we'll feel the negative consequences of that decision more intensely. Our ability to function productively will be significantly hindered which in turn will negatively impact all other areas of our lives such as relationships and work. It, therefore, goes without saying that to become the healthiest version of yourself, you'll have to understand and take better care of your body and mind. The more harmonious your mind-body connection is, the happier, energetic, productive and resilient you will be.

There's a wonderful conversation that Dr. Deepak Chopra and Oprah Winfrey had back in the '90s (when women had really strange hairstyles). And in my opinion, I think the lessons shared on that day can greatly benefit us as empaths today. Dr. Chopra taught that every person has a body type and that knowing one's body type is the easiest way to find inner balance and harmony. He went on to share the three body types and how we can know which one applies to each of us, but he also mentioned that some of us might actually be a combination of more than one. And that is okay too. Gaining an awareness of which one or two body types you are is what matters because with this knowledge you'll make better choices with your eating, exercising and resting habits.

Another critical thing that I took away from watching that conversation is something Dr. Chopra said. He said, "Whenever you react to anything whether it's a traffic jam, criticism from your boss, a love note, rainy weather, or a headache, you're really reacting not to the external signal, but to something that you generate within yourself. And if you become aware of that and you become aware of your tendencies, then you can change things in your life. Whether that's food, relationships, environment or the way you manage stress and bring about balance. So knowing your body type helps you to create more balance in your body."

That is such powerful stuff. You should probably read it repeatedly. If you have chosen to become an empowered empath, this type of insight is invaluable because it helps guide your actions and the changes that you can start making within and without. Instead of treating nutrition and exercise as an obligation, they become intentional choices you make because you have a deeper understanding of your body and the connection it has with your sense of inner harmony and well-being. Naturally, your inner harmony and well-being will become projected into outer reality. Therefore I see this topic of taking care of your diet and making sure you regularly move your body as something enjoyable. It is a lifestyle choice that continues to aid you as you grow and thrive in society.

Healthy eating habits:

This is about nourishing your body with foods and beverages that are good for your body. Foods that help you soothe your sensitivities. For empaths and highly sensitive people, we know that stimulants aren't very good for us so it would be wise to reduce or eliminate anything that over stimulates your body and sensory system. Fresh fruits and vegetables have high water content and are very rich in fiber so these should be a priority for us. They also contain antioxidants, which help keep the skin looking younger.

Omega 3 fatty acids reduce stress, and we all know how hyperactive our bodies are so it would be a good idea to include Omega 3 into your diet. I am a great fan of black tea and Vitamin C as I find it helps to reduce my stress hormones and protect my immune system, but I would recommend reducing the intake of high carbonated foods as much as possible. This isn't a book on diet, and you can find plenty of books that dive into specific diets you can try out. My intention here is to drive a simple point home: With our sensitivities, hyperactive nervous systems and all the energy we process daily, a balanced diet that works for our body type is imperative. It will prevent unhealthy food cravings, fuel us and enable us to fight off anything detrimental to our bodies.

Regularly moving your body:

Like it or not, exercise is good for your physical, mental and emotional well-being. In fact, when I skip my regular workout for an extended period, my emotions become a bit overwhelming. Exercising helps me enhance my sense of well-being, happiness, emotional balance, and my relationships. It can also be a great stress buster or a fast way of breaking negative stagnant energy that's threatening your inner peace.

Science has now proven that even a little bit of regular exercising can help you fight depression, anxiety, loneliness and it boosts self-confidence. In other words, all the negative stuff that usually keep a disempowered empath feeling stuck and miserable can be overcome by integrating regular workouts into your routine.

Now, I know what you might be thinking... "I hate going to the gym" or "I don't have an hour every day for the gym!"

This isn't about going to the gym, and it doesn't matter how much time you have. You can exercise anywhere you want. At home, at the park, in your hotel room and so on. You are limited by your level of creativity. And if you have an excellent workout routine, even twenty minutes is enough to get you going. Consider cycling, power walks, Zumba classes, Salsa lessons, martial arts, Yoga, Pilates, Cross Fit, jogging just to name a few. If traditional workouts don't work for you, find something that does. Again, going back to what Dr. Chopra said, it's about understanding yourself and what you need to find inner balance.

A great place to start knowing more about your body and what it needs is to learn more about the Ayurvedic body types, (also known as Doshas) and seeing which type feels more like you. Let me briefly share what the three body types are and how they react under stress. Then I encourage you to go research more about your Aryuvedic body type so you can see the best way to nourish and exerc

What is your Dosha or Body Type?

Vata: If you're a Vata body type then you're light, flexible and tend not to gain weight or muscle easily. You are hyper metabolic meaning you can basically eat anything you want and never gain weight. Usually very enthusiastic and full of energy but when under stress or pressure you'll quickly fall into anxiety, suffer from insomnia, have muscle spasm, migraine headaches, etc.

Pitta: If you're a Pitta then you have a muscular, athletic build. You are brave, courageous and articulate. You're like a fiery metabolic and when under stress you can get impatient, and suffer from ulcer, hypertension and heart attacks, etc.

Kapha: If you're a Kapha then you're friendly, joyful, vivacious and compassionate. You'd be considered hypo metabolic and typically tend to have extra body fat. When under stress you tend to hold on to things whether that's food, relationships, etc.

Again, this is just a brief description of each of the three doshas and by digging a little deeper using the research links provided at the end of this book. You can also do some of the simple dosha tests offered by platforms like the Chopra Center.

- Food dilemmas for empaths and highly sensitive people.

Figuring out the right diet plan or what to eat on a day-to-day basis can be quite a challenge for us, which might become overwhelming, and we don't want that. We know that if we eat too little, we'll get light headed, feel exhausted, anxious, jittery and probably crave things that aren't good for our bodies. We also know overeating is a terrible experience, so I recommend you research on the types of diets that feel interesting to you now that you understand a little more about your body type. Test out a few and modify them to fit your lifestyle. As a general rule of thumb, here's what I think works across the board.

• Build your diet around high fiber foods like fruits and vegetables. If you have things like protein, nuts, seeds, and whole grain make sure they are high quality and "sit well" with your digestion.

- Eat bigger portions at the start of the day and lower the sizes, as the day gets older. By reducing the quantity (not the quality) of your food intake as the day comes to an end, you give your body ample time to digest, and you can also use that fuel during the day when you need it most. I also find eating lighter in the evenings helps me sleep comfortably.

- Stay super hydrated throughout the day. The more hydrated you are, the sharper your brain will be, and it will help you escape the trap of snacking on junk food every hour. A great way to avoid the support of caffeinated drinks is to have more water as fatigue is directly related to dehydration. The more active you are (if working out etc.), the more water you'll need to drink that day.

- Try to avoid going on extreme crash diets or extreme detox regimes. It's okay to do a light detox from time to time, but strict juice fasts are not something I recommend. This is because such extreme fluid fasts strain the body's digestive system and organs and are quite exhausting. As an empath, this self-induced stress can be misinterpreted poorly causing the body to go into fight or flight mode instead of "detox and rest" mode.

After everything we've shared so far, I hope it is becoming clear that increasing your level of awareness is key. Becoming more aware of your body type, how your body reacts to specific foods and the types of diets and exercises that bring out the healthiest version of you is the best way to enjoy the healthy lifestyle you want. It all comes down to your willingness to self-educate and self-study so you can make better, stronger choices.

Now, let's talk about practical ways you can practice self-care daily.

Tips For Self-Care

- Practice self-forgiveness daily.

Create a customized ritual that you go through each day to self-reflect and take responsibility for your actions and energy. Taking some time each day to observe yourself as an outsider and notice how you reacted or behaved in certain situations enables you to learn and grow from your mistakes rather than unconsciously punishing yourself. This is what self-compassion is all about. Take your mistakes, mishaps, disappointments or any other scenarios where you didn't show up as your best self and reframe those mistakes as lessons. See them as your opportunity for self-discovery and growth.

• Get more sleep

Everyone needs to get adequate sleep. This is a topic that has been getting a lot of attention even in the business world with successful individuals like Arianna Huffington advocating the importance of sleeping more in a sleep-deprived society. For empaths and highly sensitive people, sleeping more is just as important as eating right and exercising. Our nervous system is hyperactive and continually working on processing all the bits and data around us. When we sleep, we have the chance to de-stress and reset the nervous system. We give it a break from all the sensory overload, giving us more power to function better the next day. Everyone is different, so you need to figure out your optimum sleep time. Most people require a minimum of 8 hours every night. Start with going to bed an hour earlier this week and take note of the change in focus, emotional stability and how rested you feel.

• Exercise.

Not everyone enjoys going to the gym, but exercising isn't about hitting the gym. It's about moving your body and breaking a sweat while enjoying it. If going to the gym doesn't excite you find something that will. Try doing Yoga, Pilates, cycling, jogging in the park, martial arts, and hula hooping or dancing. Mix things up, combine a few routines to make your own and create a routine that you can sustain as a lifestyle.

• Check in with your body at regular intervals throughout the day. This is called practicing mindfulness. Stop at intervals, breathe and acknowledge yourself. Notice how you feel in body, mind, and spirit. If you sense negativity or any kind of discomfort deal with it immediately. Don't allow things to snowball as it becomes tough to handle yourself when you stop being in charge of your inner state.

• Meditate.

This is one of the easiest ways to instantly practice self-care, ground yourself and reconnect your mind-body-spirit. Some people (including me) cannot survive a day without mediating. Others don't find it so useful. It's necessary to give it a try before assuming it won't work for you. Encourage yourself and practice some patience if you're just learning how to meditate because, for the most part, I know those who turn it into a ritual find it hard to ever go back. Meditation is so powerful because it reduces stress and creates a stronger connection with the whole of your being. It can also be a great way to go within and gain some clarity and insight when you need guidance about your life.

• Distance yourself from toxic people and toxic situations.

It's time to choose your inner circle more cautiously. Now that you understand how porous you are to your environment surround yourself with people who will uplift, encourage, inspire and support you. Gravitate toward positive people with generous, loving energy and cut down the time you spend with relatives or colleagues who don't bring out the best in you. The stronger and more empowered you become as you continue to develop yourself, the easier it will be to distance yourself physically and emotionally from those that aren't for your highest good. This will take practice and some courage especially when you realize some of the toxic people are blood relatives, but each time you step away from those dark energy spots, you'll be performing an act of self-care and self-love.

• Take time to process your emotions.

Identify and locate the emotion physically as soon as you become aware of it. Then set aside a few minutes, calm yourself and allow yourself to process what you're feeling. Make sure you choose to do this where you won't be disturbed. With your eyes closed, connect with your body and that energy; observe it first as yourself, then as an undetached detective. Witness this experience without judgment and let your attention pass through your body as you observe the sensations that are coming up. Now, express the feeling and place your hand on the part of your body where you feel that energy the strongest. For example, if it's a tight chest, place your hand on your chest and say it out loud, "it hurts here."

If you can't say it out loud, then consider writing it out on a piece of paper. Be aware that whatever you are feeling is happening inside your body and that you are fully responsible. This isn't about making yourself feel guilty, ashamed, weak or wrong. You always have the power to interpret the experience in any way you choose. Recognize that you always have the ability to respond to any adverse situation in a new and creative way. No one has power over you; not even your sensitivities. Hold this understanding in your consciousness for a few minutes as you release that energy. Continue placing your hand on that part of your body that feels discomfort and with every exhalation of your breath, have the intention of releasing that tension. Do this for the next 30 seconds. Feel the sensation leaving your body with every breath.

• Connect with nature.

American author Elizabeth Gilbert wrote a short piece entitled " Go to the Water" that I think nails this idea home for us. I know you already know the deep connection experienced when you're out in nature, but I want to encourage it even more.

Dear Ones - Years ago when I was going through a really hard time, a friend of mine who was a naturalist gave me some beautiful advice about how to best take care of myself. He told me, "when an animal in the wild has been injured, it has only two strategies for how to heal itself: It can rest, or it can go to the water. Right now, try to do as much of both as possible."

Make it a daily habit to connect with nature as much as you can. Soak in some sun, hug a tree, or if you're fortunate enough to live in a location where you can go to the water.

• Practice gratitude daily.

This is one of the most powerful rituals you can integrate into your life.

Zig Ziglar said, "Gratitude is the healthiest of all human emotions. The more you express gratitude for what you have, the more likely you will have even more to express gratitude for." I couldn't have said it better myself. If you want to become a thriving empath, this is the secret sauce that gets you there. Gratitude will shift your mood and energy instantly. Regardless of what's going on in your life or who is around you, if you can come back into the state of gratitude and focus on what you can appreciate, feel deep thankfulness for and praise then you will immediately feel the shift.

• Journal.

Get into the daily habit of being with your thoughts for a few minutes. It can be to self reflect on the day, to make intentions at the beginning of the day, to give gratitude for the things that really matter to you or a combination at different intervals. Journaling can also be a great way to help you process emotions because you can acknowledge how your feeling, name it, tame it and release it.

- Practice being in the present moment.

Most of the time we get overwhelmed or anxious because we allow our thoughts to move to a future or past event which we honestly can't control. The only time that is in your control is the time you presently have. Be more in the now and choose to do the best you can with what you've got right where you are. You'll be surprised how much power this gives you, especially when presented with a situation that threatens your peace of mind.

- Chunk down your workload and goals.

Since we know how quickly we can get overwhelmed, it becomes necessary to organize our workload and schedules in a way that promotes harmony. Planning things in advance and chunking things down further into tasks that feel small enough is actually an act of self-care. It helps you reduce procrastination and gives you the feeling of confidence needed to accomplish what you set out to do.

- Take a soothing bath.

I find this works very well for many empaths and highly sensitive people. You can take baths daily or a few times a week with your favorite salt bath and essential oils. I also like to add some scented candles and my favorite soothing music in the background just to give myself that extra treat. 30 minutes later I usually come out of that experience feeling reborn.

- Listen to music.

Music is my first love. It's my first go-to place when I need to practice self-care and self-love. I find that music has a potent effect on my mood and can aid in lowering pain, stress levels, and even my heart rate. Obviously, the type of music one listens to matters a lot; so it goes without saying, choose your music wisely. Let it be music that soothes you and brings you back to your happy place.

Chapter 06: Spirituality And Transcending Limitations As An Empath

This last chapter is devoted to those of us who are realizing that there's more to being an empath than just having a hyperactive nervous system. If you've already been studying the path of being an empath and something in you still feels like "there's more to it than what the books say," I encourage you to pay extra attention to this section. Aletheia Luna said, "One of the greatest advantages of being an empath is that experiencing a spiritual awakening is virtually inevitable. In other words, spiritually awakening seems to be written into our DNA."

We are going to shed some light on the link between being an empath and spiritual awakening. A lot of people think spirituality is wishy-washy stuff and not practical enough to be understood, but that isn't accurate. I intend to bring greater clarity into your awareness so that if you are on a path of spiritual awakening, you can quickly rise to the higher states that are even now summoning you. How will you know if there is a higher calling at play in your life? Let's start with a few signs to look out for.

• An increased and keen awareness (deep sadness and compassion) about the suffering in the world. It isn't just about your personal suffering, it's that you feel a connection with the deep despair and depression that people are experiencing in today's society.

• An increased sensation of love will also burst into your experience. You feel deep compassion for the suffering in the world, but you also feel an overwhelming love that you just want to pour into everything and everyone. You can see more clearly the world in all of its beauty not just in nature but in the people as well.

• You can feel something inside you has shifted. You're no longer the same person even though you can't fully articulate it. There's an undeniable sensation that you have become a new person; you're different, and the world seems different to you.

- Negative habits are more, and you can quickly tell what's not right in your "old life" and what must change now that you feel like a new person. Certain things that you used to tolerate or do are now intolerable. It just feels like you're ready for a change and you can't go back.

- You are experiencing insanely vivid dreams that don't make complete sense, but that give you a sense of peace. It could be that the dreams are helping pass on the insights and inner truth you've been seeking all your life.

- Synchronistic experiences happen more and more often. This means you're experiencing meaningfully related events that are too good to be a coincidence. For example, the thought of a friend you haven't seen for years crosses your mind and later that day they give you a call. You think about an old favorite song from a decade ago, and when you turn on the radio, it's the first song that plays.

These experiences tend to guide us toward a path, but sometimes, they show us to remind us that we are already on the right path.

Finding Peace And Freedom

Every human being on the planet wants to have more peace and freedom in their lives. It has increasingly become important in society as the global consciousness begins the shift from chasing after career success, money and other surface-level goals to more eternal desires. For empaths and highly sensitive people, the quest runs deeper because we already feel chained and suppressed in society. Trying to fit in, creating coping mechanisms to help us lead lives that are socially appropriate even if it's not what we desire causes us to crave freedom even more. Nothing is more elusive than peace, especially inner peace. It can feel as though forces outside your control are in charge, but this isn't fundamentally true.

To step into an experience where peace and a sense of freedom is your daily reality, you must first learn to create peace within and then all around you. The world's wisdom traditions all teach that the source of violence, war, rebellion, and unrest lies inside each of us. That includes you!

The fact that you can tune in to so many emotions and energies around you and allow them to dominate your day implies that you are using your sensitivities and gifts to perpetuate more of this dark energy. Of course, this is not to imply that it's your fault. If you haven't learned how to use your powers positively, then it's unlikely you'd be able to transcend negative energies. But when you develop yourself and become an amplifier of peace consciousness then in a very significant way, you contribute to world peace. Before you can exemplify this quality, you must first develop and embody it. The journey begins with you creating inner peace. Inner reality creates outer reality.

Dr. Deepak Chopra, an expert on this topic, tells us that finding peace and freedom begins with seeking and finding the peace that lies within. Meditation and Yoga are the tools he recommends we leverage because each of these tools enables us to look inside ourselves and create that body-mind-spirit connection.

For Dr. Chopra, this search involves transcending superficial mental activity and ordinary thinking to reach the deepest parts of our minds where peace resides. There is a place within you that is a sacred refuge; a place where you feel genuinely at peace and whole. Finding this place is a journey of a thousand miles that requires no physical effort whatsoever. Anyone can begin this journey at any point of their lives, and although it is challenging, it is well worth the mental, emotional and spiritual effort.

Here are the 4 tips Dr. Chopra shares how to do it. You'll find a link to this resource at the end of the book as well if you want to look it up and dive deeper.

Tip 1. Locate your zone of peace. This is done by going inward and transcending the constant activity of the mind.

Tip 2. Regularly return to this place of peace and make it your home. Let it be your grounding center. Whenever conditions destabilize or stress you or negative emotions come flooding in, find your way back to the zone of peace immediately. This is going to be challenging at first, but with practice, it will get easier.

Tip 3. Let go of all aspects of violence. What? I'm not into violence, I hate it! I hear you say. But the truth is, without meaning to, empaths are unconsciously participating in acts of violence. How? Resentment, entertaining negative energy, envy, anger and so on. Wasting your energy pointing fingers, feeling angry and hurt by your past, talking about energy vampires in your life and hating them for making you feel so bad is not an act of peace. Think about it for a moment. You can never fight against anything and create something positive. An angry peacemaker ceases to be a peacemaker because no peace can be found in non-peace. It's therefore vital for us as empaths to be vigilant of our egos, judgment of ourselves and others, our insecurities and the negative emotions that are active within. Dr. Chopra encourages you us to meditate until we become accustomed to the peaceful self within us who is not the ego self we know.

Tip 4. Become more intentional and allowing of your peaceful self to show up in everyday experiences. This is going to be a challenge because you encounter all types of energies and emotions. However, Dr. Chopra says that you have the power to choose to follow the silent voice of the true self and amplify that powerful peace-filled energy so much so that it drowns out the loud negative energies all around you. This requires you to stop being passive and dormant with your energy. It also requires you to release your own resentments, anger, and other emotional baggage so that the energy of love, calmness, and creativity can take over.

Be in the flow of life and let go of your imposed limitations because as long as you argue for those lower energies, you won't have access to the realm that holds the peace and freedom you yearn for. The good news is, the zone of peace is real and empowered empaths know how to prioritize it above all other experiences. Will you choose to do the same?

Spiritual awakening: The five stages

When going through a spiritual awakening, we experience emotions and energy way more than usual and at times that can be quite painful. It's like turning up the volume to full blast on your iPod while wearing your earphones. The song might be great, but your ears won't enjoy it.

As such, it's super tough to function and comfortably manage daily duties because everything is so intense and exaggerated. Add to that the natural ability to also pick up on other people's "stuff" and it's likely your awakening will feel more like a breakdown than a breakthrough.

There have been times in my life where I could have sworn things were going to hell. Nothing seemed to be moving in the direction of freedom and success that I was aiming for. My emotional and physical well-being seemed to be getting worse, not better. I was overcome with, and it made no sense whatsoever why my body felt so weak. As I connect the dots now, I can recognize (knowing what I know) that there was nothing wrong with me at all. I made it more difficult for myself by resisting it and interpreting the process poorly, so I hope by reading this, you'll avoid making that same mistake. If you're going through the motions of spiritual awakening and you're at that chaotic phase where it seems damn near impossible to maintain your sanity, rest assured that in a little while the storm will pass and you'll awaken to clear blue skies and a perfectly calm sea.

The path to freedom, wholeness, and self-healing is the path of allowing yourself to feel more. I know intense emotions usually cause us to take flight or avoid those uncomfortable feelings, but I encourage you to embrace this experience. The heightened level of sensitivities that you'll feel is what's needed to bring you back into wholeness and healing. While it can be painful, it doesn't need to be, and below I will share some of the things you can do to make this awakening process much more manageable. Before getting to that, I want to share with you a lesson that I found very useful when I started digging into this topic. Mindbodygreen.com teaches that there are 5 stages of spiritual awakening an individual goes through in their life. After going through these five teachings, I realized nothing was wrong in my life, I was simply moving from one level to the next. It helped calm my mind and trust more in the process of life. I want to share with you these five stages from the perspective of an empath and what each step will probably feel like for you.

The Change:

This is the first stage. It's when you fully realize that you really are above ordinary human awareness and that you can see, feel and experience things that others cannot. Growing up, very few of us knew that we are empaths. We ended up believing that there was something wrong with us, that we are weak and weird.

Well, the moment you awaken to the fact that you have a gift and that your sensitivities serve a purpose on this planet, you enter stage one. Awareness takes place in this first phase. You become keenly aware that you're not just crazy or making stuff up and depending on your state of mind and environment, you could feel a sense of empowerment, or you could feel totally at the mercy of other people. The energies around you increase in intensity, and you become more attuned to your gifts but probably not in a good way. For most of us, the realization that we are different makes us feel worse because we don't feel empowered enough to use this difference positively. Although it is life itself calling us to serve a higher purpose, we often get stuck in a victim mindset, and some even go around teaching it is a curse to be as we are.

The Shift:

Those of us who go through life struggling with the fact that we are aware of the differences and powers that we possess continue to observe and self-reflect. Then we get curious enough to ask a different question.

What if this is a good thing?

As soon as we start thinking along these new lines, we move into the second phase where we become conscious of this inner need to do more and be more. We start wondering if at all it is possible to make a difference in the world and contribute to the community. We seek the chance to be more proactive instead of continually being reactive. It's really hard at first, but the yearning is there to become a better person. Suffering is still part of our reality at this point, but even in the midst of it all, we sense something more is calling us.

The Search:

By the time you and I hit this stage our soul is fully connected with our intellect, and we start craving soul satisfaction. At that point, we are on fire. Like a burning bush that won't die no matter how great the storm is. That's when you would start searching for classes, videos, podcasts, books such as this one or anything else that can give you answers and guidance on how to take the next step forward.

I assume by reading this far, you're more likely in this stage of your awakening. Keep going no matter how difficult the path is because you are well on your way to unfolding the highest version of yourself. Freedom and the peace you've been yearning for all your life is within reach. The more forward momentum you create, the more you will evolve your soul and gain spiritual wisdom.

The Desire:

This is the stage where the real desires of your heart emerge and for the first time (especially after reading this book) you pay close attention to them. You listen to and attend to your needs without feeling guilty or selfish. It also becomes necessary for you to seek our new company so you might notice that you feel like surrounding yourself with like-minded souls and people who are on the same path of spiritual awakening. This is the stage where the stormy seas begin to calm down, and the real cleansing takes place. It feels natural to release any toxins, people who no longer feel right, and habits that aren't for your highest good. The best part is you'll do it with effortless ease.

The Opening:

This is the last stage after much of the cleansing and healing has taken place. It's the empowered state that every empath dreams of experiencing. At this phase of your life, freedom and peace of mind is a daily reality. You're no longer just trying to survive; you're actually thriving as an empath.

The reason this stage is called the opening is that you are more open, welcoming and in control of your power. You've learned to love and accept yourself just as you are. Instead of feeling like a victim in this world because of your powers, you feel empowered by your sensitivities almost like a superhuman because you can do, feel, experience and influence things in a way that most people can't. At this stage in your life, it becomes clear that every change, shift, and desire along this path has led you deeper into the discovery of your own soul and potential. As you finally begin to understand the greater meaning behind your life and sensitivities, you're more open to developing those gifts so that you can become a light that positively impacts this planet. Every little thing that crosses your path, all the people (yes, even the toxic people) become part of a chain to your greater good. You see the lesson that each person helped you learn and how much stronger you've grown as a result of your childhood and past experience. The story is rewritten, and you truly connect to your soul's purpose.

This is my hope for all empaths because I know how much the world needs more highly sensitive and empathic people to rise into power and shift the universal consciousness. Only through the spiritual awakening is this possible because we must first grow, develop and transcend before we can be able to illuminate the path for others. The suffering that's going on in this world won't be eradicated through force, resistance or constriction but through love and compassion.

I can't think of anyone better to start pouring this love and compassion into the world than an empowered empath, can you?

Daily spiritual practices to help you thrive

• Set daily intentions that help you develop and tap into your highest divine potential.
Choose to start each day intentionally. Always think about who you want to be that day and how you want to show up in your work, relationships and with your goals.
• Bring more awareness to the activities you engage in.
In every moment you have the power to bring in more awareness, and it is one of the best daily practices to integrate into your life should you wish to be more spiritually awakened. Ask yourself throughout the day " What am I doing now?" It's such a simple question yet so profound when it comes to bringing our full awareness into the present moment. It's a great way to take yourself out of autopilot reactions.
• Find calming scents that elevate your mood. Many empaths enjoy finding scents and using them in their surrounding daily. Some even include incense burning as part of their daily meditation routine because incense purifies the air and elevates the mood. I have a friend who carries around a small bottle with a special perfume that she takes out several times a day and rubs a few drops on her hands whenever she needs energy soothe. You can also choose to use essentials oils or scented candles depending on where you want to use them.
• Carry spiritual items such as crystal tones, necklace, etc. It can also be an inspirational note in your purse or wallet or a gratitude stone. Some people will hang a set of mala beads on the rearview mirror of the car. I like to keep my earphones close to me because I have spiritually uplifting material on my phone in the form of audio books and music. The purpose of this is to have something you can quickly fall back on the moment you feel you need some spiritual nourishment.
• Meditation. This is by far the most common practice (that even I swear by) if you want to connect with the spiritual aspect of yourself. I don't think it needs to be complicated, just start with 1-minute meditation focusing on your breathing, and as you get better at that, you can employ more advanced measures. There are also lots of apps like Head Space and Chopra Meditation Experience that can guide you through the mastery of this practice. The most important thing is to find a technique that you enjoy.

- Watch your inner dialogue. By choosing to notice the tone and nature of your internal conversation as well as the mind movies you're continually playing throughout the day, it becomes easy to change the things that don't serve you. If like most of us you realize you are your own worst enemy, you'll feel more determined to start changing how you handle yourself. And you can more intentionally welcome higher knowledge and spiritual guidance because spiritual awakening cannot happen to a mind that is waging war against itself. Remember that the next time you self-loath or self-judge.
- Invest in self-education and spiritual study. Choose to invest in educating and nourishing yourself spiritually. The same way you invest in nourishing, clothing and taking care of your physical body, you must also be interested in advancing your spiritual self. Be curious about your growth as a spiritual being. Do a self-audit every few months to see how your inner world is feeling. Find spiritual teachers, guides and material that support your growth. Choose to build that connection deliberately and expect to see inner and outer changes.
- Connect with other like-minded souls. This journey of being a spiritually awakened empath doesn't have to be a lonely one. It can be difficult at the beginning of your awakening to find people who deeply resonate with you. This is where finding a tribe and a mentor to help support you on the journey becomes invaluable. You'll need people who understand and appreciate the journey you're on. Usually, these people will be easy to connect with as you start to take yoga classes or spiritually enlightening courses so don't be shy, go out there and find those who get you. In today's digitally connected world, it has never been easier for you to find those rare gems that are just like you.

Next Steps

While empaths are warm, intuitive, and compassionate people, their high level of sensitivity makes them prone to experiencing issues such as anxiety, depression, and crippling physical illnesses. The journey isn't necessarily easy if you were born to be an empath, but the good news is, you have what it takes to be an illuminating light in this world.

The first step is gaining awareness about yourself and learning what your blind spots are so you can start avoiding the traps that have been sabotaging your life so far. You've got to be courageous enough to step out of your comfort zone. Leave behind the old patterns, traumas, and lies that you've had to grow up with and step into a more liberated version of yourself. I believe this book has taken some huge strides in showing you exactly how you can step out of the victim mindset that many of us get stuck in and into a state of empowerment.

What you possess is a gift and although you may not understand it fully at this point, trust in the process of life. Learn how to develop yourself so you can stop feeling drained of your precious energy. It's time to deal with the challenges of being a highly sensitive empath in a way that empowers you and transforms the lives of those around you. It might be that life has been one continuous struggle, but from this point on, you hold the power to bring into reality a life of significant meaning filled with joy, love, great health, and success. The world needs that special gift that only you have.

Resources

Highly sensitive people Tips For Survival: https://www.psychologytoday.com/intl/blog/prescriptions-life/201105/top-10-survival-tips-the-highly-sensitive-person-hsp

Healing emotional trauma: http://www.chopratreatmentcenter.com/blog/2018/04/26/5-simple-steps-healing-emotional-trauma/

Meditation for beginners: https://chopra.com/articles/start-here-5-meditation-styles-for-beginners

Finding your Dosha: https://yogainternational.com/article/view/dosha-quiz

www.ingramcontent.com/pod-product-compliance
Lightning Source LLC
Chambersburg PA
CBHW081154070526
44583CB00021B/2828